TERRORISM
RESPONSE
Field Guide for Fire and EMS Organizations

PAUL M. MANISCALCO MPA, Ph.D. (C), EMT/P

HANK T. CHRISTEN, MPA, EMT/B

D1469159

Prentice
Hall

10 9 8 7 6 5 4 3 2 1

Please visit our web site at www.pearsoned.com

ISBN 0-13-110906-5

BA 996219

 PEARSON EDUCATION
75 Arlington Street, Suite 300, Boston, MA 02116
A Pearson Education Company

Contents

In Loving Memory of:

Henry T. Christen Sr.

Judson Fuller

Anthony S. Maniscalco

"The final test of a leader is that he leaves behind him in other men the conviction and the will to carry on and succeed."

—WALTER LIPPMAN

About the Authors

Paul M. Maniscalco MPA, PH.D.(C) EMT/P

Paul M. Maniscalco is an Adjunct Assistant Professor with The George Washington University and a Deputy Chief Paramedic for one of the largest urban EMS systems in the world. His previous commands include: Field Response, Command and Management assignments in the Communications Division, Training Division, Field Services Bureau, Office of the Chief of Operations and Commander of the Special Operations Division. Chief Maniscalco has over 25 years of Public Safety response, supervisory and management experience. During his tenure he has had the responsibility of responding to and managing a wide array of events ranging from aviation & rapid transit emergencies, natural disasters to civil disturbances and acts of terrorism. Chief Maniscalco has also been engaged in command roles for managing special events such as dignitary visits, national political conventions and a wide variety of mass gatherings.

Paul has lectured extensively and is widely published in academic & professional journals on Emergency Medical Service, fire service, special operations, public safety and national security issues. He is the co-author of the Brady textbook *"The EMS Incident Management System: EMS Operations for Mass Casualty and High Impact Incidents,"* a contributing author to the Chemical and Biological Arms Control Institutes *"Hype or Reality? The 'New Terrorism' and Mass Casualty Attacks",* the US Fire Administrations *"Guide to Developing and Managing an Emergency Service Infection Control Program",* National Fire Service Incident Management System Consortiums *"Model Procedures Guide for Emergency Medical Incidents, First Edition",* International Federation of Red Cross/Red Crescent Societies and Johns Hopkins School of Hygiene and Public Health-Center for Disaster and Refugee Studies *"Public Health Guide for Emergencies"* and also the co-author of *"Understanding Terrorism and Managing the Consequences"* (Prentice Hall/Brady).

Chief Maniscalco is a member of the Department of Defense, Defense Science Board, Transnational Threat Study and the Homeland Defense–Chemical Weapons Task Force; the Department of Defense, Interagency Board (IAB) EMS/Medical Working Group and an Advisor to the Defense Advanced Research Project Agency ENCOMPASS project. Additionally, Maniscalco holds an appointment to the Harvard University, John F. Kennedy School of Government and Department of Justice Executive Session on Domestic Preparedness, a three-year panel examining the issues of responding to acts of terrorism. He is also an appointee to the United States Congressionally mandated National Panel to Assess Domestic Preparedness (Gilmore Commission) and sits as the Chairman of the State and Local Response Panel.

Paul M. Maniscalco earned his Baccalaureate degree in Public Administration–Public Health & Safety from the City University of New York, a Master of Public Administration–Foreign Policy & National Security from the New York University Wagner Graduate School of Public Service. He is presently a candidate for a Doctoral Degree in Organizational Behavior with a focus on disaster management.

Henry T. Christen, MPA, EMT

Hank Christen, is the Director of Emergency Response Operations for Unconventional Concepts Inc. He was previously a Battalion Chief on the Atlanta Fire Department, and Director of Emergency Services, Okaloosa County, Florida.

He has served as the Unit Commander for the Gulf Coast Disaster Medical Assistance Team and responded to national level disasters including multiple hurricanes, wildfires, and the 1996 Olympics under the Federal Response plan.

He is a member of the Department of Defense, Defense Science Board, Transnational Threat Study and has served on the Department of Defense, Interagency Board (IAB) EMS/Medical Working Group and an Advisor to the Defense Advanced Research Project Agency. He is currently a member of the Executive Session on Domestic Preparedness, John F. Kennedy School of Government, Harvard University.

Hank has been a speaker at international disaster conferences since the 1970's, is a contributing Editor to *Firehouse Magazine,* and has published over 50 technical articles. He is the co-author of *The EMS Incident Management System—A Guide to Mass Casualty and High Impact Events* (Brady, 1998) and a contributing author for the International Federation of Red Cross/Red Crescent Societies and Johns Hopkins School of Hygiene and Public Health-Center for Disaster and Refugee Studies *"Public Health Guide for Emergencies".* He is also the co-author of *Understanding Terrorism and Managing Consequences* and *Terrorism Response—Field Guide for Law Enforcement* (Prentice Hall/Brady).

Contributors & Reviewers

The authors would like to thank the following contributors to our project. Their invaluable assistance and expertise enhanced the overall quality of our end product. They are:

Frank J. Cilluffo
Director, Terrorism Task Force
Chairman, Chemical, Biological, Radiological, Nuclear (CBRN) Task
   Force
Center for Strategic and International Studies
Washington, D.C.

David Cid
Asst. Special Agent in Charge
Federal Bureau of Investigation
Oklahoma City, Okalhoma

James P. Denney MA, EMT/P
Executive Director
Global Emergency Management Services Association
Alta Loma, CA
Principal
Organizational Strategic Solutions (OSS) Group

Gerald F. Dickens EMT-D (retired)
Hazardous Materials Technician
Logistics Coordinator
Special Operations Division
New York City Emergency Medical Service

Neal J. Dolan MCJ, NREMT-P
Special Agent in Charge
United States Secret Service

Michael J. Hopmeier MSME
Chief, Innovative and Unconventional Concepts
Unconventional Concepts, Incorporated
Eglin Air Force Base, Florida

Dennis R. Krebs CRT
Captain, Baltimore County Fire Department
International Survival Systems
Baltimore, Maryland

Michael V. Malone
Major, United States Marine Corps.

Susan S. McElrath MS(c), BSHP
McElrath and Associates
Powder Springs, Georgia

Eugene J. O'Neill NREMT-B
Rescue Specialist
WMD/Domestic Preparedness Lead Instructor
Special Operations Group
University Hospital EMS, Newark, New Jersey

Frederick R. Sidell MD
Former Chief, Chemical Casualty Care Office
Former Director, Medical Management of Chemical Casualties Course
U.S. Army Medical Research Institute of Chemical Defense
Aberdeen Proving Ground
Chemical Casualty Consultant
Bel Air, Maryland

Charles E. Stewart MD, FACEP
Emergency Physician
Colorado Springs, Colorado

Robert L. Walker
Explosive Ordinance Disposal
Subject Matter Expert
Ft. Walton Beach, Florida

Introduction

Terrorism and tactical violence incidents are most times, first and foremost a high impact multiple casualty incident. This means that EMS and Fire agencies are directly involved in every response aspect for the consequences created by these heinous actions. Fire and EMS have the responsibility for saving lives, protecting property and conserving the environment (in that priority order). The lessons of the past vividly point to the dangers of responding to a terrorist incident. It is imperative that EMS and Fire response organizations assure that their response and operational doctrines properly prepare their members for the significant challenges that Fire Fighters and EMS personnel will confront.

Terrorism and tactical violence incidents present a myriad of challenges for the Emergency Responder. First, responders will confront a violent, dangerous, and unstable scene that can kill them. Secondly, they may face new chemical, biological, and radiological threats with little (or no) protective equipment or training for this continually changing threat. Lastly, a successful attack will result in mass casualties and multiple fatalities. This complex combination of threats and high impact aftermath make these scenes unlike anything most of us have ever responded to before. These unknown or unfamiliar environments we may enter, only serve to amplify the dangers we will be required to work around in order to safely discharge our duties and save lives.

The purpose of this pocket guide is to provide a quick reference of Fire and EMS regarding consequence management responsibilities during a terrorist attack. Most importantly, it is a safety guide to help members survive.

Paul M. Maniscalco

Hank Christen

Chapter 1

The Basics of the Incident Management System

IMS Management Structure

- ☆ Incident manager and management staff
    - Public information officer
    - Liaison officer
    - Safety officer
- ☆ Operations officer
    - Operations branches—Fire/rescue, EMS/Health, Law Enforcement
- ☆ Logistics officer
    - Communications, supply, food/water, facilities, and ground support units
- ☆ Planning officer
    - Situation, resource, demobilization, and technical advisor units

IMS Functional Sections

- ☆ Incident manager—authority for incident management; assumes all responsibilities not delegated
- ☆ Liaison officer—point of contact for assisting and coordinating agencies
- ☆ Logistics section—supervises support branch (facilities, ground support) and service branch (communications, food/water)
- ☆ Operations section—supervises operations branches; develops operational strategy
- ☆ Planning section—supervises resource, situation, demobilization, and technical advisor units; prepares incident action plan

IMS Position Definitions

- ☆ Public Information Officer—coordinates media operations functions and media briefings with the incident manager
- ☆ Resource unit—tracks incident resources and records unit status
- ☆ Safety officer—supervises incident safety operations; develops safety plan
- ☆ Situation Unit—analyzes situation as it progresses in coordination with the planning section
- ☆ Supply unit—provides personnel equipment, and supplies

IMS Structure Definitions

- ☆ Branch—IMS level having functional or geographic responsibilities; between section and division/group
- ☆ Chain of command—flow of orders/information from management levels to subordinate levels in the IMS
- ☆ Management staff—incident manager's support staff; liaison, safety, and public information units
- ☆ Section chief—command level between incident manager and branches
- ☆ Sector officer—supervises members performing similar functions/tasks; example SWAT, triage, decontamination, etc.
- ☆ Span of control—number of subordinate units that can be effectively managed; usually 3 to 5 units in emergency operations
- ☆ Strike team—Up to 5 of the same kind of resources with a single leader
- ☆ Task force—Up to 5 unlike resources assembled for a specific mission with a common leader

Fire/Rescue IMS

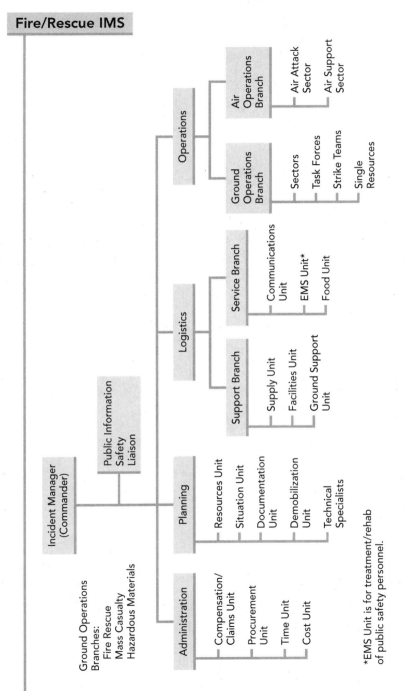

By Paul M. Maniscalco and Hank T. Christen, reprinted from *Mass Casualty and High-Impact Incidents: An Operations Guide* (2002), Prentice-Hall, Inc.

Emergency Medical IMS

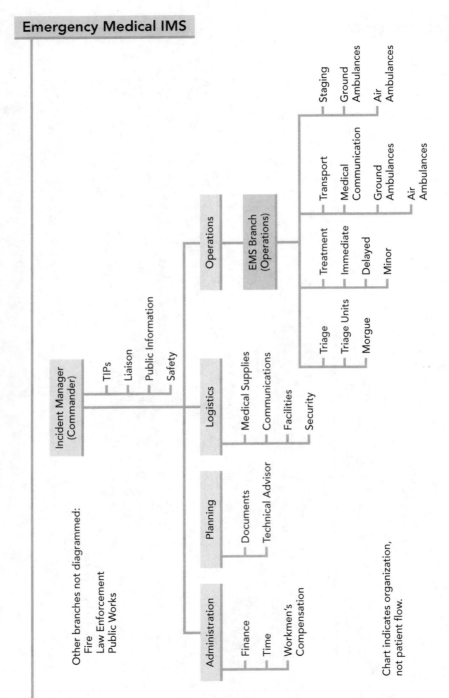

By Paul M. Maniscalco and Hank T. Christen, reprinted from *Mass Casualty and High-Impact Incidents: An Operations Guide* (2002), Prentice-Hall, Inc.

Law Enforcement IMS

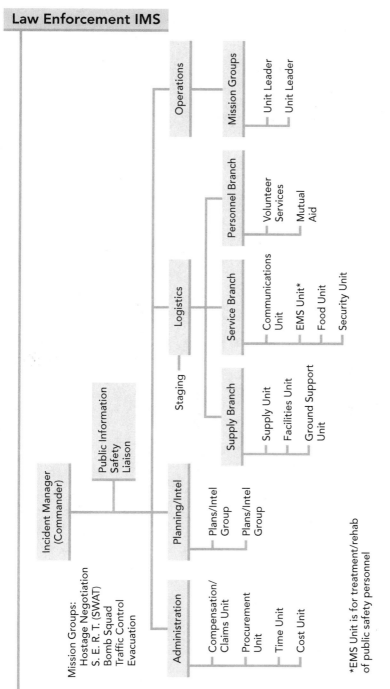

By Paul M. Maniscalco and Hank T. Christen, reprinted from *Mass Casualty and High-Impact Incidents: An Operations Guide* (2002), Prentice-Hall, Inc.

Public Works IMS

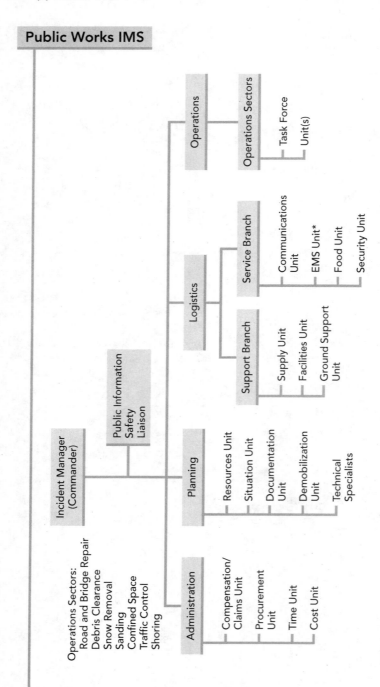

By Paul M. Maniscalco and Hank T. Christen, reprinted from *Mass Casualty and High-Impact Incidents: An Operations Guide* (2002), Prentice-Hall, Inc.

The Safety Template

The most important duty of the incident manager is safety. A safety officer must be assigned whenever an incident manager cannot directly supervise all safety aspects of the incident.

 The safety officer has the authority to temporarily suspend any plan or tactical action that is unsafe.

On long duration incidents, the safety officer writes the formal safety plan and conducts safety briefings in coordination with the incident manager and the planning section chief.

Specialized safety functions include:

1. Traffic safety
2. Weapons safety
3. Landing zone safety
4. EMS infection control
5. Haz mat safety officer
6. Personnel accountability officer
7. SWAT team safety officer
8. Fire/rescue safety officer
9. Special team safety (water, high angle, and confined space rescue)
10. Radiation safety officer
11. Explosives safety
12. Biological safety officer

Military Coordination

Major terrorism incidents involve coordination with military and/or National Guard units. The military refers to IMS as "command and control."

The primary functions of military command and control systems are:

★ Commander (equivalent to IMS incident manager)
★ S-1 Administration (equivalent to IMS administration section chief)
★ S-2 Intelligence (equivalent to IMS planning section chief)
★ S-3 Plans/operations (equivalent to IMS operations section chief)
★ S-4 Logistics (equivalent to IMS logistics section chief)

Note: "S" stands for staff

There are two primary methods for the integration of civilian and military units:

1. Unified command—the military commander and the incident manager jointly share command responsibilities.
2. Section/Branch assignment—a military unit is assigned (by joint agreement) to operate in an appropriate IMS section or branch (example: a military medical unit is assigned to the EMS/medical branch)

Push Logistics Package

- ★ Personal protective equipment—suits and respiratory equipment
- ★ Decontamination equipment
- ★ Medications—EMS drugs and antidotes
- ★ Morgue supplies—body bags, collection bags, tags
- ★ Medical supplies—life support and trauma supplies
- ★ Weapons—special issued weapons and ammunition
- ★ Crime scene supplies—evidence bags, photo equipment, forms
- ★ Detection equipment—chemical, biological, radiological, and explosives
- ★ Scene control equipment—markers, cones, signs and scene tape
- ★ Incident command cache—vests, checklists, forms

Chapter 2

Response Procedures for Terrorism and Tactical Violence Incidents

Convergent Responders

Convergent responders are citizens or individuals from non-emergency agencies that witness a terrorism/tactical violence event and "converge" on the scene.

These organizations include:

1. Utility crews such as power, gas, telephone and cable
2. Postal workers and express delivery services (like FedEx or UPS)
3. Meter readers and inspectors
4. Transit authority, school buses and taxis.
5. Public works crews
6. Social workers or probation officers
7. Private security agencies
8. Real estate agents
9. Crime watch and neighborhood watch volunteers
10. Truck drivers

Many of these people are in radio-equipped vehicles or have cellular telephones and can provide early and accurate reports of a suspicious scene or a terrorism/tactical violence event in progress.

Scene awareness principles begin before the response in any incident (routine or terrorism). Being familiar with the neighborhood, the surroundings, and the violence history of the area is important. For example:

* Does the location or area have a past history of events or attempted incidents?
* Are special events being held?

11

★ Has a warning been issued for the immediate area or vicinity?

★ Is the stadium full or empty?

★ Has there been recent unrest such as political protests or union/labor issues?

★ Are special religious ceremonies being held?

During an **emergency response,** scene awareness jumps into high gear.

★ While responding, mentally explore the possibility that the scene may be far worse than the initial information.

★ Monitor the radio traffic; turn up the volume and really LISTEN.

★ Know the wind direction.

When you get close enough for the scene to appear in the distance, start really looking.

★ Visually scan the entire scene periphery (this may be limited at night or bad weather).

★ Force yourself to look around the incident.

★ If you see threats to your safety, or if you have a "sixth sense" that something is wrong, stop and even retreat. Always trust your "sixth sense" on the street.

★ When exiting your vehicles look for indications of an unsafe scene.

★ Start looking above, behind you, and for bad guys on roofs.

★ Look for any indication of people with weapons, explosive devices, or evidence of a chemical agent.

Critical Factor: Do not become blinded by "Tunnel Vision." Survey the entire scene including above for threats to your safety

The "2 in 2 out" principle

Fire service procedure requiring two members to enter a hot zone; two other members remain in a standby position for rescue. This principle can apply to law enforcement in a terrorism/tactical violence incident when the scene is unstable.

DON'T LEAVE YOUR PARTNER!

LACES principle:

L—lookout; someone is responsible for watching the overall scene from a safe distance and warning crews of danger.

A—awareness; all members on the scene have situational awareness and are ready for unpleasant surprises.

C—communications; exposed crews must have effective communications which includes direct voice or hand signals as well as portable radios.

E—escape; plan an escape route and an alternate route from any unstable scene

S—safety zones; escape to a safe area that provides distance, shielding, and upwind protection.

New Scenes, New Surprises

1. On a bombing, suspect a partially exploded device or a second device.
2. Coordinate scene security with the law enforcement agency having jurisdiction.
3. If a second device is found or suspected, evacuate one thousand feet in every direction (including above).
4. Patients should be removed as if they were in a burning vehicle; use minimal spinal precautions and omit invasive procedures until patients are in a safe area.

Chemical Incident Response

First responders must look for indicators and remember several important points:

1. Suspect a chemical agent if you are presented with several non-trauma patients with like symptoms.
2. Check for patients that may be scattered throughout a crowd or facility.
3. Look for convergent responders that are showing symptoms; beware of direct exposure or transfer of mechanisms of injury from patients to responders.
4. Does the patient area smell funny or unusual?
5. In extreme cases, a forward bodyline indicates the hot zone (no man's land).
6. Listen for radio traffic from other units indicating multiple patients.
7. Establish a hot zone fast; get the walking patients out.
8. Call for special teams quickly; control hot zone entry.

The First Arriving Unit

No matter where you fit in the management hierarchy, someone has to get there first. The first arriving unit has a drastic effect (positive or negative) on the progress of the incident). Remember the key principle of IMS:

Scene management builds from the bottom up.

This means the first arriving unit is the incident manager, and is responsible for operations, logistics, and planning.

- ★ Requesting assistance is the first priority.
- ★ Make a quick scene survey and transmit a radio report.
- ★ In the initial report give your command post location (remember you are the incident manager at this point) and a basic description and establish a staging location that is in a safe area.
- ★ Don't leave your vehicle until you get feedback confirming reception.
- ★ If the event is a non-violent mass casualty incident, your partner or crewmembers can begin triage efforts.
- ★ If the event is terrorism/tactical violence, stay with your partner ("2 in 2 out").
- ★ Try to determine the scope of the hot zone, an approximate number of patients, and a mechanism of injury.

It is critical that you transmit scene threats over the dispatch radio system. Make sure dispatchers relay this information to other units and agencies. This includes information such as:

1. Shooters on the scene or perpetrators with weapons.
2. A suspicious device(s).
3. A possible CBRNE hot zone.

Finally, command is relinquished by the first due unit when a senior officer, supervisor or manager arrives. This process is done face-to-face and announced over the dispatch radio channel.

Scene Control

The objective of scene control is to establish a secure perimeter around the scene/hot zone for the purpose of controlling entry and exit from the incident area. Entry control prevents civilians or media from converging on the area. Effective scene control also establishes entry points where personnel and units are logged in for accountability purposes.

Keeping people in the hot zone from leaving the scene is a new scene control issue unfamiliar to most of us. In a chemical, biological or radiological incident, it is important to keep victims in an casualty collection or evacuation area. This decision is made by medical personnel or a hazardous materials officer (consult local protocols). We do not want contaminated victims spreading the mechanism of injury.

Scene Control Solutions

☆ Hospitals throughout the region should be alerted. The importance of decontamination before admission must be stressed.

☆ On-site monitoring determines the extent of the hot zone. The perimeter is reduced accordingly.

☆ A strong law enforcement perimeter must be established around the crime area. All evidence must be properly preserved, photographed, cataloged, and removed.

☆ Scene entry points are established for public safety personnel to control warm zone and hot zone access. A local personnel accountability system must be effectively utilized.

☆ All receiving hospitals must initiate entry control procedures. Contaminated vehicles are diverted to a remote and secured parking lot (not the ER driveway). Arriving patients are diverted to a decon area outside the building for clothing removal and initial washdown. No patient is permitted entry into any hospital area without being decontaminated.

☆ 911 calls outside the incident area are handled by a beefed up response force of mutual aid units and recall personnel. Records from all exposed patients are separately maintained for inclusion into a final after action report. All cases are also reported to law enforcement for future investigation.

☆ The media may be instructed to establish a media pool. The media pool may be given a closely supervised escorted tour of areas cleared by the safety officer and law enforcement and authorized by the Incident Manager.

Medical Facility Response

A terrorism/tactical violence incident requires medical facilities to alter their general mode of operations and respond to the demands of the event. The initial element in hospital preparation that drives the rest of the hospital response system is communications. Medical receiving facilities must be alerted early in the event chain. Communications are assured (at least have a high potential for success) by correct protocol and multi-layers of technology. As EMS communications transmits scene information, medical facilities must be in the receiving loop.

Hospital security is a key non-medical element in hospital response. Hospital security should be immediately alerted when mass terrorism/tactical violence victims are being transported to the facility. Armed officers should secure entry to the emergency department (ED) and related treatment areas.

Contaminated patients in route to an ED require a different type of security plan. Security should initiate a complete facility lock down. If the decon area is separate from the ED entrance, security must be positioned to direct arriving vehicles (EMS and private cars) to the decon corridor. Security checklists and protocol for each guard should be written in a pocket guide format and issued to each security officer especially rotation guards.

> **Critical Factor:** Hospital/Medical Facilities MUST adopt terrorism incident protocols within their disaster plans as well as secure the necessary equipment to support actions related to these type events. Reliance upon local emergency response agencies to augment hospital capacity to manage patient load or decontamination is unwise. We discourage this dependency based upon the understanding that most, if not all, emergency assets will be either committed to the management of the incident (at the site) or sustaining 911 operations for calls unrelated to the terrorism incident.

Summary

The Top Ten Response Issues of Terrorism Tactical Violence are:

1. Fire and EMS agencies are the cornerstone of an effective terrorism/ tactical violence response. Plan to be self-sustaining for twelve to twenty four hours before federal help arrives.
2. Convergent responders arrive before "first responders." Identify convergent responder agencies and develop an awareness-training program for them.
3. A terrorism/tactical violence scene is definitely a hostile workplace environment. Focusing on victims instead of an overall scene awareness can get you killed. Use your senses; look around before charging in. Beware of a chemical hot zone, shooters in the area, and primary or secondary explosive devices.
4. Use the buddy system when entering an unsecured scene by applying the "2 in 2 out" principle. Also apply the wildland firefighting principle of LACES: lookout, awareness, communications, escape and safety zone.

5. A trend of mass shootings and tactical ultra-violence means more exposure to ballistic hot zones. Examine the peripheral areas of a scene, including roofs or other high places. Use the principle of distance and cover for self-protection. (If you're debating about ducking and running you should have already been doing it!)
6. The incident management system (IMS) is the boilerplate for management of terrorism/tactical violence incidents. Learn it, implement it, train on it, exercise it, and use it.
7. Scene control is a critical factor in a terrorism/tactical violence event and has high impact on law enforcement. Victims, witnesses, and possible assailants must be kept on the scene. Other groups will attempt to enter the scene such as media, onlookers, friends and families of the victims.
8. All emergency responders must be specially trained for terrorism/tactical violence incidents. This includes IMS proficiency, scene awareness, and special team training.
9. Medical facilities must initiate response protocols for processing and treating mass casualty terrorism/tactical violence patients. Facility response begins with effective communications to provide early scene information.
10. Hospital security is a major factor in medical facility preparedness. The ED must be protected. In a chemical or radiation incident, patients must be decontaminated before entry; the facility must be "locked-down."

Chapter 3

Weapons of Mass Effect— Chemical Terrorism

WARNING: Fire and EMS personnel should never enter a chemical hot zone without proper certification and protective equipment. In most cases, these functions are performed by fire/rescue agencies. Consult local protocols.

WARNING: The medical protocols described in this section are for reference only and are beyond the scope of training for non-medically certified firefighters. Officers should immediately call for EMS support as dictated by local protocols.

> **Critical Factor:** Fire and EMS agencies must be prepared for a consequence response to a chemical attack.

Nerve Agents

Nerve agents are toxic substances that produce incapacitation, injury and death within seconds to minutes. The signs and symptoms caused by nerve agent vapor are characteristic of the agents and are not difficult to recognize with a high index of suspicion. Effective antidotes are available for use that will save lives and reduce injury if administered in a timely manner.

Nerve agents are a group of chemicals similar to, but more toxic than, commonly used insecticides, such as Malathion or Parathion.

NERVE AGENTS

- ☆ Block the activity of an enzyme
- ☆ Cause too much neurotransmitter
- ☆ Cause too much activity in many organs
    - glands
    - muscles
    - skeletal muscles
    - smooth muscles (in internal organs)
    - other nerves

NERVE AGENT EFFECTS

Glands
- ☆ lachrymal (tearing)
- ☆ nose (runny)
- ☆ mouth (salivation)
- ☆ sweat (increased to profuse)
- ☆ bronchial (in airways)
- ☆ gastrointestinal

Skeletal muscles
- ☆ fasciculation, twitching, weakness, paralysis

Smooth muscles
- ☆ airways (constriction)
- ☆ gastrointestinal (cramps, vomiting, diarrhea)

Central nervous system
- ☆ loss of consciousness
- ☆ convulsions
- ☆ cessation of breathing

VAPOR EXPOSURE

Small concentration
- ★ miosis (red eyes, pain, blurring, nausea)
- ★ runny nose
- ★ shortness of breath

Effects start within seconds of contact

Large concentration
- ★ loss of consciousness
- ★ convulsions
- ★ cessation of breathing
- ★ flaccid paralysis

Effects start within seconds of contact

LIQUID ON SKIN

Very small droplet
- ★ sweating, fasciculation
- ★ can start as long as 18 hours after contact

Small droplet
- ★ vomiting, diarrhea
- ★ can start as long as 18 hours after contact

Lethal-sized droplet or larger
- ★ loss of consciousness
- ★ convulsions
- ★ cessation of breathing
- ★ flaccid paralysis
- ★ usually starts without warning within 30 minutes

Removing the patient from the area of contamination, or the vapor area, would be rather simple in a normal hazmat incident, but the complexities of a mass casualty terrorism event present some unique challenges. If the agent was released inside a building or other enclosed space moving the patients outside should suffice.

Patients should be relocated far upwind from the source. Removal of agent from skin must be done as early as possible, and before help can arrive. It is unlikely that you will see a living patient with visible amounts of nerve agent on his skin.

> **Critical Factor:** Treatment for nerve agent exposure involves decontamination, administration of antidotes, and ventilation.

INITIAL ANTIDOTE USE

Vapor exposure
☆ Miosis and/or runny nose
    no antidotes unless eye pain is severe (eye drops)
☆ Shortness of breath
    2 or 4 mg of atropine depending on severity; 2-PAMCl by slow drip
☆ Unconscious, convulsions, severe breathing difficulty; moderate to severe effects in two or more systems
    6 mg of atropine IM; 2-PAMCl by slow drip; ventilation

Liquid on skin
☆ Localized sweating, fasciculation
    2 mg of atropine; 2-PAMCl by slow drip
☆ Vomiting, diarrhea
    2 mg of atropine; 2-PAMCl by slow drip
☆ Unconscious, convulsing, severe breathing difficulty; moderate to severe effects in two or more systems
    6 mg of atropine IM; 2-PAMCl by slow drip; ventilation

In all cases: follow with 2 mg of atropine every 5 to 10 minutes until improvement occurs

Cyanide

Cyanide, like the nerve agents, can cause serious illness and death within minutes. Cyanide was not successful as a warfare agent in World War I for several reasons; (a) it is very volatile and tended to evaporate and be blown away by a breeze, (b) it is lighter than air and will not stay close to the ground where it can do damage, and (c) the dose to cause effects is relatively large and, unlike other agents, it causes few effects at lower doses.

CYANIDE—LARGE AMOUNT BY INHALATION

Hyperventilation:	15 seconds
Convulsions:	30 seconds
Cessation of breathing:	3–5 minutes
Cessation of heartbeat:	6–10 minutes

CYANIDE—MANAGEMENT

Amyl nitrite perle
Sodium nitrite IV (10 ml; 300 mg)
Sodium thiosulfate IV (50 ml; 12.5 gm)

Ventilation with oxygen
Correction of acidosis

Critical Factor: Cyanide antidotes are amyl nitrites, sodium nitrite, and thiosulfate.

Vesicants

Vesicants are things that cause vesicles or blisters. They may be of animal, vegetable, or mineral origin, such as some types of sea creatures, poison ivy, and certain chemicals. Other things, such as sunlight, can produce blisters. Vesicants have been used as chemical warfare agents. Several have been developed for this purpose, but only one, sulfur mustard, has been used. The other major chemical warfare vesicant is Lewisite.

Critical Factor: Vesicants cause vesicles or "blisters."

MUSTARD—INITIAL EFFECTS

No immediate effects; effects start hours after contact

Skin
- ⭐ redness (erythema) with burning and itching
- ⭐ blisters

Eye
- ⭐ redness with burning and itching

Airways
- ⭐ nasal and sinus pain
- ⭐ sore throat, non-productive cough

Critical Factor: Immediate decontamination is very important with mustard exposure.

Lewisite

Lewisite is an oily liquid with the odor of geraniums. Its freezing point is below 0°F, it boils at 190°F, it contains arsenic, a heavy metal, and it is more volatile than mustard. An important initial clinical distinction between Lewisite and mustard is that Lewisite vapor causes immediate irritation of eyes, skin and upper airways. Lewisite liquid causes pain or burning on whatever surface it contacts within seconds. The patient is alerted to its presence and will leave the area or remove the liquid. Mustard causes no clinical effects until the lesions develop, hours after contact.

Pulmonary Agents

Pulmonary agents are chemicals that produce pulmonary edema (fluid in the lung) with little damage to the airways or other tissues. The best known and most studied of these is phosgene (carbonyl chloride), although other chemicals, e.g., chlorine, behave in this manner.

PULMONARY AGENTS—INITIAL EFFECTS

No immediate effects; effects begin hours after exposure

★ shortness of breath with exertion, later at rest
★ cough, later with production of frothy sputum

If many patients are complaining of irritation or burning in the eyes and nose, on the mucous membranes of the mouth, and on the skin, one might consider

a. riot control agents (in which case the patients will improve with fresh air),
b. phosgene (this effect will improve, but there will be later, more severe ones),
c. cyanogen chloride (the irritation will gradually decrease and if the patient is conscious when help arrives it is unlikely that a lethal concentration was present), or
d. Lewisite (the effects will worsen).

TABLE 3-1 Chemical Agents: Symptoms and Treatment

Nerve Agents (GA, GB, GD, GF, VX)	Mustard (HD, H)
Signs and Symptoms: Vapor: *Small exposure*—Miosis, rhinorrhea, and mild dyspnea. *Large exposures*—Sudden loss of consciousness, convulsions, apnea, flaccid paralysis, copious secretions, and miosis. Liquid on skin: *Small to moderate exposure*—Localized sweating, nausea, vomiting, and feeling of weakness. *Large exposure*—Sudden loss of consciousness, convulsions, apnea, flaccid paralysis, and copious secretions.	**Signs and Symptoms:** Asymptomatic latent period (hours). Erythema and blisters on the skin, irritation, conjunctivitis, corneal opacity, and damage in the eyes; mild upper respiratory signs, marked airway damage; also gastrointestinal effects and bone marrow stem cell suppression.
Decontamination: Large amounts of water with a hypochlorite solution.	**Decontamination:** Large amounts of water with a hypochlorite solution.
Immediate Treatment/Management: Administration of atropine and pralidoxime chloride (2PAM); diazepam in addition if casualty is severe; ventilation and suction of airway for respiratory distress.	**Immediate Treatment/Management:** Decontamination immediately after exposure is the only way to prevent/limit injury/damage. Symptomatic management of lesions.
Lewisite (L)	**Phosgene Oxime (CX)**
Signs and Symptoms: Lewisite causes immediate pain or irritation of skin and mucous membranes. Erythema and blisters on the skin and eyes and airway damage similar to those seen after mustard exposure develop later.	**Signs and Symptoms:** Immediate burning and irritation followed by wheal-like skin lesions and eye and airway damage.
Decontamination: Large amounts of water with a hypochlorite solution.	**Decontamination:** Large amounts of water.
Immediate Treatment/Management: Immediate decontamination; symptomatic management of lesions the same as for mustard lesions; a specific antidote British Anti-Lewisite (BAL) will decrease systemic effects.	**Immediate Treatment/Management:** Immediate decontamination; symptomatic management of lesions.

TABLE 3-1 Continued

Cyanide (AC, CK)	Pulmonary Agents (CG)
Signs and Symptoms: Few. After exposure to high estimated dose (Ct): seizures, respiratory and cardiac arrest.	**Signs and Symptoms:** Eye and airway irritation, dyspnea, chest tightness, and delayed pulmonary edema.
Decontamination: Skin decontamination is usually not necessary because agents are highly volatile. Wet, contaminated clothing should be removed and the underlying skin decontaminated with water or other standard decontaminates.	**Decontamination:** Vapor: fresh air. Liquid: copious water irrigation.
Treatment: Antidote intravenous sodium nitrite and sodium thiosulfate. Supportive care: oxygen and correct acidosis.	**Treatment:** Termination of exposure, ABCs of resuscitation, enforced rest and observation, oxygen with or without positive airway pressure for signs of respiratory distress, other supportive therapy as needed.

Riot Control Agents (CS, CN)

Signs and Symptoms:
Burning and pain on exposed mucous membranes and skin, eye pain and tearing, burning nostrils, respiratory discomfort, and tingling of the exposed skin.

Decontamination:
Eyes: thoroughly flush with water, saline or similar substance. *Skin:* flush with copious amounts of water, alkaline soap and water, or a mildly alkaline solution (sodium bicarbonate or sodium carbonate). Generally decontamination is not required if wind is brisk.

Treatment:
Usually none is necessary; effects are self-limiting.

Source: *Medical Management of Chemical Casualties Handbook,* 2nd edition, Chemical Casualty Care Office, United States Army Medical Research Institute of Chemical Defense, Aberdeen Proving Ground, Maryland, 1995.

Summary

It is essential that Fire and EMS agencies be prepared for a chemical attack. Effective planning must include protective equipment, decontamination procedures, and antidotes. A deliberate incident is a crime scene, usually with mass numbers of patients. Each patient is an actual or potential witness to the crime that has taken place.

Nerve agents are toxic substances that produce incapacitation, injury and death within seconds to minutes. Effective antidotes are available for use that will save lives and reduce injury if administered in a timely manner.

Vesicants are agents that cause vesicles, or "blisters." The most common vesicant agents are sulfur mustard and Lewisite. Mustard does not cause an immediate effect; the common latent period is four to eight hours after contact. Inhaled vapor causes damage to the airway and bronchioles. Patients must be decontaminated immediately and the eyes irrigated.

Lewisite produces instant effect on contact. The symptoms include immediate pain, eye damage, and airway injury.

Pulmonary agents produce pulmonary edema. The best-known agents are phosgene and chlorine. The effects of these agents are not immediate, but shortness of breath followed by pulmonary edema follows hours after exposure. Exposed patients with no symptoms must be kept under medical observation for at least six hours. Initial patient treatment includes keeping the patient at rest and administering oxygen.

Riot control agents are known as tear gas and irritants. They include CS (tear gas), CN (Mace), and pepper spray. Effects begin in seconds, but last only a few minutes after the patient is removed to fresh air. These agents cause pain, burning, and irritation to the contact body surfaces.

Within our society there are many different chemicals that are accessible to rogue individuals and organizations to exploit for use against our communities. While this section reviews the "military" variations of chemical weapons, law enforcement officers need to remain cognizant of the technology "blow-back" that could be yielded via the release of toxic industrial chemicals and materials found in many communities.

Critical Factor: Upon arrival at any scene, survey the location and if a hazardous materials release is suspected:

- ☆ Evacuate the area
- ☆ Deny entry to non-essential personnel
- ☆ Position yourself upwind and up-hill from the source

Chapter 4

Weapons of Mass Effect— Biological Terrorism

WARNING: Fire and EMS personnel should never enter a biological hot zone without proper certification and protective equipment. In most cases, these functions are performed by fire/rescue agencies. Consult local protocols.

WARNING: The medical protocols described in this section are for reference only and may exceed the scope of training for non-medically certified fire fighters. Fire fighters should immediately call for EMS & Public Health support as dictated by local protocols.

Introduction

Biological terrorism is the use of etiological agents (disease) to cause harm or kill a population, food, and/or livestock. Biological terrorism includes the use of organisms such as bacteria, viruses, and rickettsia and the use of products of organisms—toxins.

Biological terrorism has recently become more threatening to the world. One only needs to consider the current state of technology, the future possibilities of bio-technologies and what appears to be a readiness of some individuals / countries to utilize this technology as a weapon.

Personnel Protective Equipment

Biological terrorism is most likely to be executed covertly and sick individuals may be the initial "detector" that an attack has occurred. If delivered "effectively" a large number of casualties can be generated in a short period of time. In the midst of treating all of the casualties, the emergency responder and organization must not only provide effective care, but also protect themselves and their members.

Emergency medical service, fire, police, and even hospitals must purchase PPE and train employees for work in protective gear that has only been found in the military and specialized hazardous materials teams. Emergency service organizations must realize that they are significant targets for primary/secondary attacks and conduct their routine operations appropriately while ensuring that the proper security measures are implemented.

Threat Assessment

INTELLIGENCE: When a BW manufacturing facility can be constructed in the area of a large garage, law enforcement/intelligence services are confronted with a great difficulty locating them. As has been noted, most of these agents are not "controlled" and can be found endemically throughout the world. Accessing cultures is not nearly as expensive or tracked as well as nuclear material. BW culture processing requires equipment that would be considered suitable for a well-equipped hospital laboratory or academic research facility, and thus easily ordered and diverted. If this does not sound credible, please note that Saddam Hussein bought his original anthrax cultures from a mail order house in the United States and had it shipped by a commercial overnight carrier.

DETECTION: Detection of biological agents is most often after a release. Quite simply, there is no way to detect the deployment of a bacterial agent in the civilian community under normal operating procedures and presently available technology for civilian use. The only way to detect the agent is through the clinical presentation of patients, and that will be retrospective for most of the casualties. Some limited battlefield detection devices exist, but these are unusable in the majority of United States cities. These devices are effective for special events such as the Olympics, Inauguration, or where crowds are moderately constrained but due to cost and availability has limited benefit to the local emergency response organizations. When threat assessments are quite high and advance notice of that threat exists, access of these items through the National Guard WMD Civil Support Teams or through DoD is highly recommended.

Biological warfare agents are almost undetectable during transit. Likewise, there is no mechanism using routine customs, immigration, drug scan, or bomb search procedures to identify the agent. The only way to find it would be a physical search by a very well trained and very lucky searcher. Indeed, the agent could be simply sent using FedEx or similar overnight carrier from one point to another. Even in an event where a package is broken and product is leaked, in essence you have a high index of suspicion, identification of the agent will usually take place at a laboratory not in the field.

Response time

Even if an astute emergency physician notes that an unusual number of patients have X symptoms and contacts the CDC for help, the crisis is recognized immediately as a bio-terrorism event, and help is dispatched immediately, the lag time may be unwieldy. Remember that with some of the agents that have been identified, there is an incubation period that exceeds 3 days from time of agent distribution until the first cases occur and some agents bring with them a 20 day period. The patient may be quite infective during latter parts of this incubation period with emergency personnel and hospital staff unaware of the jeopardy they are in. The mortality rate approaches 100 percent when symptoms present with some of these agents.

Given an absolute best-case scenario from notification, it will take at least 2 hours for a qualified team of pre-designated physicians and pre-hospital providers (paramedics & EMTs) to assemble (if a community has had the foresight to convene a team prior to the event), ready gear, and respond to the deployment assembly point.

It will take another few hours to assess the situation, draw appropriate clinical samples, and formulate an idea of what illness or toxin was employed. During this time, others will be exposed and potential carriers may be leaving the city bound for other destinations.

Botulinum toxins

Botulinum neurotoxin is among the most potent toxins known. The mouse lethal dose is less than 0.1 nanograms per 100 grams. It is over 275 times more toxic than cyanide.

Mueller (1735–1793) and Kerner (1786–1862) in Germany first described botulism. They associated the disease with ingestion of insufficiently cooked "blood sausages" and described death by muscle paralysis and suffocation. In the early

1900s, botulism occurred commonly in the United States and nearly destroyed the canned food industry.

Clostridium toxins

Tetanus neurotoxin is secreted by Clostridium species in similar fashion to botulinum. The intoxication occurs at extremely low concentrations of toxin, is irreversible, and like botulism, requires activity of the nerve to cause toxicity to that nerve.

Clostridium perfringens also secretes at least 12 toxins and can produce gas gangrene (clostridial myonecrosis), enteritis necroticans, and clostridium food poisoning. One or more of these toxins could be produced as a weapon. The alpha toxin is a highly toxic phospholipase that could be lethal when delivered as an aerosol.

Ricin

Ricin is a type II ribosome inactivating protein produced by the castor bean plant and secreted in the castor seeds. The toxin is a 576 amino acid protein precursor weighing 65000 Daltons. Once inside the cell, ricin depurinates an adenine from rRNA and thereby inactivates the ribosome, killing the cell.

Ricin is available worldwide by simple chemical process of the castor bean. Although ricin is only a natural product of the castor bean plant, ricin has been produced from transgenic tobacco using gene transfer principles. Large amounts of toxin would be able to be produced easily by this transgenic method.

Saxitoxin

Saxitoxin is a dinoflagellate toxin responsible for paralytic shellfish poisoning. It is also found in several species of puffers and other marine animals and was originally discovered in 1927. The toxin is very soluble in water, heat stable and is not destroyed by cooking. The lethal dose is 1–2 mg. There are multiple related toxins with substitutions at key positions.

Staphylococcal enterotoxin

Staphylococcal food poisoning is familiar to emergency physicians. The disease is changed when the enterotoxin is delivered by aerosol. The organism that produces this agent is readily available and could be tailored to produce large quantities of the toxin.

Tetrodotoxin

Tetrodotoxin is a potent neurotoxin produced by fish, salamanders, frogs, octopus, starfish, and mollusks, notably the puffer (also called the globefish or blowfish). The dangers of tetrodotoxin poisoning were known by the ancient Egyptians (2400 to 2700 BC). All organs of the fresh water puffer are toxic with the skin having the highest toxicity followed by gonad, muscle, liver, and intestine. In salt water puffers, the liver is the most toxic organ. The lethal dose of tetrodotoxin is only 5 micrograms per kilogram in the guinea pig.

Possible live bacteriologic warfare agents

This list covers only a few diseases that have been researched. Much information was obtained from The United States Army Field Manual 8–9; Handbook on the medical aspects of NBC defensive operations (FM 8–9), Part II—Biological United States Government Printing Office:1996 also available on the internet as http://www.nbc-med.org/FMs. Other diseases have been proposed and researched as a result of multiple sessions with interested colleagues or my travels to the city of Sverdlovsk in the USSR.

Although these diseases have been proposed by the United States military and others as possible biologic warfare agents, there is no question that the list is neither exhaustive nor all inclusive. Other diseases that have been considered include typhoid fever, Ebola virus, melioidosis, Rift Valley fever, epidemic typhus, Rocky Mountain Spotted fever, scrub typhus, coccidiomycosis, histoplasmosis, ChikunGunya fever, Congo Crimean fever, lassa fever, dengue fever, Eastern equine encephalitis, Western equine encephalitis, Venezuelan encephalitis, Omsk hemorrhagic fever, Korean hemorrhagic fever and many others (at least 60). The astute reader can recognize the potential for biowarfare in almost any disease that can possibly afflict humans. Numerous other diseases could be used as biowarfare agents against selected crops or livestock.

Anthrax

Anthrax is caused by *Bacillus anthracis*. Under usual (non-wartime) conditions, humans become infected by contact with an infected animal or contaminated animal byproducts. Anthrax is also known as "wool-sorter's disease." There are three forms of anthrax: cutaneous, inhalation, and gastrointestinal. Almost all naturally occurring cases of anthrax are cutaneous or gastrointestinal. During the 2001 anthrax attacks, the fatalities resulted from inhalation anthrax.

Anthrax is likely to be disseminated as an aerosol of the very persistent spores. The incubation time is from one to six days, anthrax may have a prolonged incubation period of up to two months. The longer incubation periods are seen most frequently when partial treatment has been given. The spores can be quite stable, even in the alveolus. The duration of the disease is between two and five days.

Brucellosis

Brucellosis is a zoonotic disease caused by a small non-motile coccobacilli. The natural reservoir is domestic herbivores such as goats, sheep, cattle, and pigs. There are four species: *Brucella melitensis, B. abortus* (cattle), *B. suis* (pigs), and *B. canis* (dogs). Humans become infected when they ingest raw infected meat or milk, inhale contaminated aerosols, or through skin contact. Human infection is also called undulant fever. Human to human transmission is rare if it occurs at all.

Brucella species have been long considered as biological warfare agents because of the stability, persistence, and ease of infection without human to human transfer. Brucellosis can be spread by aerosol spray or by contamination of food supply (sabotage). There is a long persistence in wet ground or food.

Cholera

Cholera is a well known diarrheal disease caused by *Vibrio cholera* acquired in humans through ingestion of contaminated water. The organism causes a profound secretory "rice water" diarrhea by elaborating an enterotoxin.

Although cholera can be spread by aerosols, more likely terrorist or military employment would be contamination of food or water supplies. There is negligible direct human to human transmissibility. The bacterium does not have long persistence in food or pure water and not persistent when applied by aerosols.

Ebola virus

The Ebola virus is a member of a family of RNA viruses known as filoviruses. When magnified several thousand times by an electron microscope, these viruses have the appearance of long filaments or threads. Ebola virus was discovered in 1976 and was named for a river in Zaire, Africa, where it was first detected.

Ebola virus has been covered significantly in the popular literature and in several books and movies (*Outbreak*). The Aum Shirinkyo cult visited Zaire to collect Ebola. This virus is well spread by body fluids, particularly blood. It is quite dangerous for the health care provider because human-to-human contact will rapidly spread the disease. It is capable of aerosol spread.

Use of this virus (with greater than 90% lethality) would be considered a "doomsday" operation by the military. There is no guarantee that this virus would be able to be contained if spread to a modern city. The persistence is low, but the transmissibility is so high that this is immaterial.

Plague

Plague is a zoonotic disease caused by *Yersinia pestis*. It is naturally found on rodents and prairie dogs and their fleas. Under normal conditions three syndromes are recognized: inhalational (pneumonic), septicemic, and bubonic. The usual first infection is the bubonic form.

In 1994, defectors revealed that the Russians had conducted research on *Yersinia pestis*, the plague bacterium to make it more virulent and stable in the environment. The plague can retain viability in water for 2 to 30 days, moist areas for up to 2 years, and in near freezing temperatures for several months to a year.

Plague could be spread by either infected vectors such as fleas, or by an aerosol spray. Person to person transmissibility is high and the bacterium is highly infective. The persistence is low, but the transmissibility is so high that this is immaterial.

Q fever

Q fever is a rickettsial zoonotic disease caused by *Coxiella burnetti*. The usual animals affected are sheep, cattle, and goats. Human disease is usually caused by inhalation of particles contaminated with *Coxiella*.

Q fever is a self-limiting febrile illness of 2 days to 2 weeks. The incubation period is about 10 to 20 days. The patient is usually ill, but uneventful recovery is the rule. Q fever pneumonia is a frequent complication and may be noted only on radiographs in most cases. Some patients will have nonproductive cough and pleuritic chest pain. Other complications are not common and may include chronic hepatitis, endocarditis, meningitis, encephalitis, and osteomyelitis.

Smallpox

Smallpox has been used as a biologic weapon in the United States during the French and Indian War. Smallpox is an orthopox virus which affects primates, particularly man. The disease was declared eradicated in the world in 1977, and the last reported human case occurred in a laboratory in 1978. Theoretically, the virus exists in only 2 laboratories in the world in the United States and in Russia. The virus can be transmitted by face to face contact, secretions, and aerosols. It is a durable virus and can exist for long periods outside the host. It is remotely possible that it is still living outside of the repository labs. A very closely related disease, Monkeypox, cannot be easily distinguished from smallpox.

Smallpox has a long incubation period of about 10 to 17 days. The illness has a prodrome of 2–3 days with malaise, fever, headache, and backache. Over the next 7 to 10 days, all of the the characteristic lesions erupt, progress from macules to papules to vesicles to pustules and then crust and scarify. The lesions are more numerous on the extremities and face than on the trunk. The disease is fatal in about 35% of cases. Some patients will develop disseminated intravascular coagulopathy. Other complications include smallpox pneumonia, arthritis (may have permanent joint deformities) and keratitis (may cause blindness).

Tularemia

Tularemia or "rabbit fever" is caused by Francisella tularensis, a gram negative bacillus. Humans can contract this disease by handling an infected animal or by the bite of ticks, mosquitoes, or deerflies. The natural disease has a mortality rate of 5–10%. As few as 50 organisms can cause disease if inhaled.

The following tables are for reference only. Law enforcement officers should not attempt diagnosis or treatment. The primary law enforcement mission is scene control, evidence preservation and support of EMS and public health operations. *Biological evidence should only be obtained by trained biological recovery teams that have certified PPE.*

TABLE 4-1 Biological Agents: Symptoms and Treatment

Anthrax	Cholera
Signs and Symptoms: Incubation period is 1–6 days. Fever, malaise, fatigue, cough, and mild chest discomfort are followed by severe respiratory distress with dyspnea, diaphoresis, stridor, and cyanosis. Shock and death occur within 24–36 hours of severe symptoms.	**Signs and Symptoms:** Incubation period is 1–5 days. Asymptomatic to severe with sudden onset. Vomiting, abdominal distention, and pain with little or no fever followed rapidly by diarrhea. Fluid losses may exceed 5–10 liters per day. Without treatment, death may result from severe dehydration, hypovolemia, and shock.
Diagnosis: Physical findings are nonspecific. Possible widened mediastinum. Detectable Gram stain of the blood and by blood culture in the course of illness.	**Diagnosis:** Clinical diagnosis; Watery diarrhea and dehydration. Microscopic exam of stool samples reveals few or no red or white cells. Can be identified in stool by dark field or phase contrast microscopy and can be grown on a variety of culture media.
Treatment: Although usually not effective after symptoms are present, high dose antibiotic treatment with penicillin, ciprofloxacin, or doxycycline should be undertaken. Supportive therapy may be necessary.	**Treatment:** Fluid and electrolyte replacement. Antibiotics such as tetracycline, ampicillin, or trimethoprim-sulfamethoxazole will shorten the duration of diarrhea.
Prophylaxis: A licensed vaccine for use in those considered at risk for exposure. Vaccine schedule is 0, 2, and 4 weeks for initial series, followed by boosts at 6, 12, and 18 months, and then a yearly booster.	**Prophylaxis:** A licensed, killed vaccine is available, but provides only about 50% protection that lasts no more than 6 months. Vaccination schedule is at 0 and 4 weeks with booster doses every 6 months.
Decontamination: Secretion and lesion precautions should be practiced. After an invasive procedure or autopsy is performed, the instruments and area used should be thoroughly decontaminated with a sporicidal agent such as iodine or chlorine.	**Decontamination:** Personal contact rarely causes infection; however, enteric precautions and careful hand washing should be frequently employed. Bactericidal solutions such as hypochlorite would provide adequate decontamination.

TABLE 4-1 Continued

Plague	Tularemia
Signs and Symptoms:	**Signs and Symptoms:**
Pneumonic plague: Incubation period is 2–3 days. High fever, chills, hemoptysis, toxemia, progressing rapidly to dyspnea, stridor, and cyanosis. Death results from respiratory failure, circulatory collapse, and bleeding diathesis. Bubonic plague: Incubation period is 2–10 days. Malaise, high fever, and tender lymph nodes (buboes); may progress spontaneously to the septicemic form, with spread to the central nervous system, lungs, and elsewhere.	Ulceroglandular tularemia presents with a local ulcer and regional lymphadenopathy, fever, chills, headache, and malaise. Typhoidal or septicemic tularemia presents with fever, headache, malaise, substernal discomfort, prostration, weight loss, and a nonproductive cough.
Diagnosis:	**Diagnosis:**
Clinical diagnosis. A presumptive diagnosis can be made by Gram or Wayson stain of lymph node aspirates, sputum, or cerebral spinal fluid. Plague can also be cultured.	Clinical diagnosis; Physical findings are usually nonspecific. Chest x-ray may reveal pneumonic process, mediastinal lymphadenopathy or pleural effusion. Routine culture is possible but difficult. The diagnosis can be established by serology.
Treatment:	**Treatment:**
Early administration of antibiotics is very effective. Supportive therapy for pneumonic and septicemic forms is required.	Administration of antibiotics with early treatment is very effective.
Prophylaxis:	**Prophylaxis:**
A licensed, killed vaccine is available. Initial dose followed by a second smaller dose 1–3 months later, and a third 3–6 months later. A booster dose is given at 6, 12, and 18 months, and then every 1–2 years. This vaccine may not protect against aerosol exposure.	A live attenuated vaccine is available as an investigational new drug. It is administered once by scarification. A two-week course of tetracycline is effective as prophylaxis when given after exposure.
Decontamination:	**Decontamination:**
Secretion and lesion precautions with bubonic plague should be practiced. Strict isolation of patients with pneumonic plague. Heat, disinfectants, and exposure to sunlight render bacteria harmless.	Secretion and lesion precautions should be practiced. Strict isolation of patients is not required. Organisms are relatively easy to render harmless by heat and disinfectants.

TABLE 4-1   Continued

Q Fever	Smallpox
Signs and Symptoms: Fever, cough, and pleuritic chest pain may occur as early as 10 days after exposure. Patients are not generally critically ill and the illness lasts from 2 days to 2 weeks.	**Signs and Symptoms:** Clinical manifestation begins acutely with malaise, fever, rigors, vomiting, headache, and backache. 2–3 days later lesions appear, which quickly progress from macules to papules and eventually pustular vesicles. They are more abundant on the extremities and face and develop synchronously.
Diagnosis: Q fever is not a clinically distinctive illness and may resemble a viral illness or other types of atypical pneumonia. The diagnosis is confirmed serologically.	**Diagnosis:** Tests of electron and light microscopy are not capable of discriminating variola from vaccinia, monkeypox, or cowpox. The new PCR diagnostics techniques may be more accurate in discriminating between variola and other orthopox viruses.
Treatment: Q fever is generally a self-limiting illness even without treatment. Tetracycline or doxycycline are the treatments of choice and are orally administered for 5–7 days. Q fever endocarditis (rare) is much more difficult to treat.	**Treatment:** At present there is no effective chemotherapy and treatment of a clinical case remains supportive.
Prophylaxis: Treatment with tetracycline during the incubation period may delay but not prevent the onset of symptoms. An activated whole-cell vaccine is effective in eliciting protection against exposure, but severe local reactions to this vaccine may be seen in those who already possess immunity.	**Prophylaxis:** Immediate vaccination or revaccination should be undertaken for all personnel exposed. Vaccinia-immune globulin (VIG) is of value in postexposure prophylaxis of smallpox when given within the first week following exposure, and with vaccination.
Decontamination: Patients who are exposed to Q fever by aerosol do not present a risk for secondary contamination or re-aerosolization of the organism. Decontamination is accomplished with soap and water or by the use of weak (0.5%) hypochlorite solutions.	**Decontamination:** Strict quarantine with respiratory isolation for a minimum of 16–17 days following exposure for all contacts. Patients should be considered infectious until all scabs separate.

TABLE 4-1 Continued

Venezuelan Equine Encephalitis	Viral Hemorrhagic Fevers
Signs and Symptoms: Sudden onset of illness with general malaise, spiking fevers, rigors, severe headache, photophobia, and myalgias. Nausea, vomiting, cough, sore throat, and diarrhea may follow. Full recovery takes 1–2 weeks.	**Signs and Symptoms:** Viral hemorrhagic fevers (VHFs) are febrile illnesses that can be complicated by easy bleeding, petechiae, hypotension, and even shock, flushing of the face and chest, and edema. Constitutional symptoms such as malaise, myalgias, headache, vomiting, and diarrhea may occur in any hemorrhagic fevers.
Diagnosis: Clinical diagnosis; Physical findings are usually nonspecific. The white blood cell count often shows a striking leukopenia and lymphopenia. Virus isolation may be made from serum, and in some cases throat swab specimens.	**Diagnosis:** Clinical diagnosis; Watery diarrhea and dehydration. Microscopic exam of stool samples reveals few or no red or white cells. Can be identified in stool by dark field or phase contrast microscopy and can be grown on a variety of culture media.
Treatment: Supportive therapy only.	**Treatment:** Intensive supportive care may be required. Antiviral therapy with ribavirin may be useful in several of these infections. Convalescent plasma may be effective in Argentine hemorrhagic fever.
Prophylaxis: A live, attenuated vaccine is available as an investigational new drug. A second, formalin-inactivated killed vaccine is available for boosting antibody titers in those initially receiving the live vaccine.	**Prophylaxis:** The only licensed VHF vaccine is yellow fever vaccine. Prophylactic ribavirin may be effective for Lassa fever, Rift Valley fever, Congo-Crimean hemorrhagic fever (CCHF) and possibly hemorrhagic fever with renal syndrome (HFRS).
Decontamination: Blood and body fluid precautions (body substance isolation {BSI}) should be employed. Human cases are infectious for mosquitoes for at least 72 hours. The virus can be destroyed by heat (80°C (176°F) for 30 minutes) and ordinary disinfectants.	**Decontamination:** Decontamination with hypochlorite or phenolic disinfectant. Isolation measures and barrier nursing procedures are indicated.

TABLE 4-1   Continued

Botulinum Toxins	Staphylococcal Enterotoxin B
Signs and Symptoms: Ptosis, generalized weakness, dizziness, dry mouth and throat, blurred vision and diplopia, dysarthia, dysphonia, and dysphagia followed by symmetrical descending flaccid paralysis and development of respiratory failure. Symptoms begin as early as 24–36 hours, but may take several days after inhalation of toxin.	**Signs and Symptoms:** From 3–12 hours after aerosol exposure, sudden onset of fever, chills, headache, myalgia, and nonproductive cough. Some patients may develop shortness of breath and retrosternal chest pain. Fever may last 2–5 days, and cough may persist up to 4 weeks. Patients may also present with nausea, vomiting, and diarrhea if they swallow the toxin. Higher exposure levels can lead to septic shock and death.
Diagnosis: Clinical diagnosis; No routine laboratory findings. Bio-terrorism/warfare should be suspected if numerous collocated casualties have progressive descending bulbar, muscular, and respiratory weakness.	**Diagnosis:** Clinical diagnosis; Patient presents with a febrile respiratory syndrome without chest x-ray (CXR) abnormalities. Large numbers of patients presenting with typical symptoms and signs of SEB pulmonary exposure would suggest an intentional attack with this toxin.
Treatment: Intubation and ventilatory assistance for respiratory failure. Tracheostomy may be required. Administration of botulinum antitoxin (IND product) may prevent or decrease progression to respiratory failure and hasten recovery.	**Treatment:** Treatment is limited to supportive care. Artificial ventilation might be needed for very severe cases and attention to fluid management is essential.
Prophylaxis: Pentavalent toxoid (types A, B, C, D, and E) is available as an IND product for those at high risk of exposure.	**Prophylaxis:** Use of protective mask. There is currently no vaccine available to prevent SEB intoxication.
Decontamination: Hypochlorite (0.5% for 10–15 minutes) and/or soap and water. Toxin is not dermally active and secondary aerosols are not a hazard from patients.	**Decontamination:** Hypochlorite (0.5% for 10–15 minutes) and/or soap and water. Destroy any food that may have been contaminated.

TABLE 4-1 Continued

Ricin	Trichothecene Mycotoxins (T2)
Signs and Symptoms:	**Signs and Symptoms:**
Weakness, fever, cough, and hypothermia about 36 hours after aerosol exposure, followed in the next 12 hours by hypotension and cardiovascular collapse.	Exposure causes skin pain, pruritus, redness, vesicles, necrosis, and sloughing of epidermis. Effects on the airway include nose and throat pain, nasal discharge, itching, and sneezing, cough, dyspnea, wheezing, chest pain, and hemoptysis. Toxin also produces effects after ingestion or eye contact. Severe poisoning results in prostration, weakness, ataxia, collapse, shock, and death.
Diagnosis:	**Diagnosis:**
Signs and symptoms noted above in large numbers of geographically clustered patients could suggest an exposure to aerosolized ricin. The rapid time course to severe symptoms and death would be unusual for infectious agents. Laboratory findings are nonspecific except for specific serum ELISA. Acute and convalescent sera should be collected.	Should be suspected if an aerosol attack occurs in the form of "yellow rain" with droplets of yellow fluid contaminating clothes and the environment. Confirmation requires testing of blood, tissue, and environmental samples.
Treatment:	**Treatment:**
Patient management is supportive. Presently there is no available antitoxin. Gastric decontamination measures should be employed if the toxin is ingested.	There is no specific antidote. Superactive charcoal should be given orally if swallowed.
Prophylaxis:	**Prophylaxis:**
Presently there is no vaccine or prophylactic antitoxin available for human use. Use of a protective mask (respirator) is currently the best protection against inhalation if an attack/exposure is anticipated.	The only defense is to wear personal protective equipment during an attack. No specific immunotherapy or chemotherapy is available for use in the field.
Decontamination:	**Decontamination:**
Weak hypochlorite solutions and/or soap and water can decontaminate skin surfaces. Ricin is not volatile, so secondary aerosols are generally not a danger to health care providers.	Outer garments should be removed and exposed skin should be decontaminated with soap and water. Eye exposure should be treated by copious saline irrigation. Once decontamination is complete, isolation is not required.

Source: Medical Management of Biological Casualties Handbook, 2nd edition, United States Army Medical Research Institute of Infectious Diseases, Ft. Detrick, Fredrick, Maryland, 1996.

Chapter 5

Weapons of Mass Effect— Radiological Terrorism

Characteristics of Radiation

Despite the similarities to hazmat incidents, radiation incidents have an unique characteristic that first responders must understand. The primary difference between a radiation incident and a hazmat (or chemical or biological) incident is that radiation exposure may occur without coming in direct contact with the source of radiation. In order to be exposed to hazmat (or chemical or biological agents), the material must be inhaled, ingested, injected, absorbed through the skin, deposited on unprotected skin, or be introduced onto or into the body by some means. Exposure to radiation, however, does not require the body to come into direct contact with the radiation source.

> **Critical Factor:** Direct contact is not needed for a radiation exposure to occur.

To understand the mechanism for radiation exposure an explanation of *radiation* is necessary. Many people incorrectly think radiation is a mysterious chemical substance. Although chemicals may be *radioactive*—they emit radiation—radiation itself is simply energy in the form of invisible electromagnetic waves or extremely small, energetic particles. Waveforms of radiation are x-ray and gamma ray. Particle forms are alpha, beta, and neutron. X-ray machines manufacture radiation and similar equipment commonly found in medical and industrial facilities and it is emitted by a wide variety of radioactive materials such as uranium and plutonium.

In facilities that use radioactive materials the standard radioactive symbol is used to label the materials so they can be readily identified. Special placards are also required for transporting certain quantities or types of radioactive materials. This information is useful when considering response to an accident involving radioactive materials. However, when considering a terrorist event you cannot rely on the presence of labels or placards to help identify the hazards involved.

Radiation Effects on the Body

No matter the form or the source of the radiation, radiation energy is deposited in the body when the body is exposed to it. The amount of energy deposited in the body by a radiation source varies widely. It depends largely on the energy of the radiation involved, its penetrating ability, and whether or not the source of radiation is located outside or inside the body. Exposure to radiation from a source outside the body is known as *external exposure.* Exposure to radiation from a source within the body is known as *internal exposure.*

Radioactive contamination is the presence of radioactive material in a location where it is not desired. Radioactive contamination results from the spillage, leakage, or other dispersal of unsealed radioactive material. The presence of radioactive contamination always presents an internal exposure hazard because of the relative ease at which it can be incorporated into the body. Depending on the radioactive material involved, it may also present an external exposure hazard.

Exposure is the irradiation of any object, living or inanimate. The term *RAD* is the unit of measure for radiation exposure. It is an acronym for *Radiation Absorbed Dose.* An exposure of one RAD results in the absorption of 100 ergs of energy per gram of tissue exposed. In the international system of units the unit of exposure is the Gray. One Gray equals 100 RAD.

The term *dose* must now be introduced to further discuss radiation's effects on living persons. *Radiation dose* is a calculated measurement of the amount of energy deposited in the body by the radiation to which the person is exposed. The unit of dose is the *REM.* It is an acronym for *Roentgen Equivalent Man. Roentgen* is another unit for radiation exposure (but it is not necessary to define the term in order to explain the concept of dose). The *REM* is derived from this unit of measure by taking into account the type of radiation producing the exposure. In the international system of units the unit of radiation dose is the *Sievert.* One Sievert equals 100 REM.

Radiation Measurements

Some instruments can measure the dose over a period of time. These can be compared to an odometer, which measures total miles traveled regardless of the speed. Though hand-held survey instruments may have this capability, they are more useful in an emergency situation to be used to measure the exposure rate. Radiation dosimeters, however, are useful to measure the exposure received over time. Personnel responding to an incident wear dosimeters. Dosimeters may be checked frequently to determine the exposure received by a first responder at an incident scene.

Survey instruments and dosimeters have certain limitations. Like all electronic equipment, survey instruments may drift over time. They should be recalibrated and inspected at regular intervals. Survey instruments also use batteries that must be checked and replaced when necessary. Dosimeters must be zeroed and checked on a regular basis. Survey instruments and dosimeters are useless if they are not functioning properly.

Health effects of radiation exposure have been studied for years. No one will argue that at high levels of exposure, serious health effects occur. These effects are called *prompt* or *acute* effects because they manifest themselves within hours, days, or weeks of the exposure. Acute effects include death, destruction of bone marrow, incapacitation of the digestive and nervous systems, sterility, and birth defects in children exposed in-utero. A localized high exposure could result in severe localized damage requiring amputation of the affected area. These effects are clearly evident at high exposures such as those produced by an atomic bomb detonation or serious accident involving radioactive materials. These effects are seen at short-term exposures of about 25 RAD and above. The severity and onset of the effect is proportionate to the exposure. Effects of radiation exposure that are not manifest within a short period of time are called *latent* or *delayed* effects. The most important latent effect is a statistically significant increase in the incidence of cancer in populations exposed to high levels of radiation.

The health effects of low exposures are not obvious and are subject to wide debate in scientific and academic circles. Low exposures do not cause obvious bone marrow damage or digestive or nervous system effects. They have not been shown to cause cancer or birth defects. Localized low exposures to the hands and feet, and arms and legs do not cause obvious harm.

Information from persons exposed to high levels of radiation has been used to predict possible health effects to persons exposed to low levels. The primary concern is the incidence of cancer. Since high exposures cause a statistically significant increase in the incidence of cancer, low-level exposure are thought to possibly cause an increase in the risk of cancer; perhaps proportionate to the increase seen at high exposures, perhaps disproportionate. To minimize risks, occupational dose limits for persons who work with radiation are set at 5 REM per year. This is not a dividing line between a safe and unsafe dose, it is a conservative limit set to minimize risk.

The basis for the "common sense, healthy respect" approach to radiation exposure held by many scientists, academics, and radiation safety professionals is a solid one.

External radiation exposure A person exposed to even a lethal dose of radiation generally presents no hazard to the individuals around him. The patient is not radioactive, and is no different from the patient who has been exposed to diagnostic x-rays. [The only exception to this rule would be the person who has been exposed to significantly high amounts of neutron radiation. Persons or objects subjected to neutron radiation may become radioactive themselves. Such activation is extremely rare and noted here for information purposes only.]

> **Critical Factor:** Minimize exposure, but avoid extraordinary measures to avoid all exposures.

External contamination The individual who has external contamination presents a different situation. Problems associated with this type of patient are similar to those encountered with chemical contamination. The presence of external contamination usually means the individual has come in contact with loose or unconfined radioactive material, such as a liquid or powder or airborne particles from a radioactive source. The objective should be containment to avoid spreading the contamination. Anyone or anything coming in contact with a person or an object that is contaminated becomes radioactive and must be considered as being contaminated until proven otherwise. Isolation techniques should be implemented to confine the contamination and protect personnel.

Internal contamination The patient who has been externally contaminated may also have received internal contamination by inhalation or ingestion. Internal contamination, however, is usually not a hazard to the individuals around the patient. The most common type of internal contamination involves the inhalation of airborne radioactive particles that are deposited in the lungs. Also possible is the absorption through the skin of radioactive liquids or the entry of radioactive material through an open wound. In all instances, there may be little or no residual surface or external contamination, but the patient may suffer the effects of exposure from the ingested or absorbed radioactive material.

Fire/EMS Considerations—Terrorism Situations

Another potential source of contamination and/or exposure that must be considered involves the deliberate dispersal of radioactive material by terrorists. The Oklahoma City federal building and World Trade Center bombings (1993 & 2001), the subway poison gas attack in Japan, the use of chemical and biological agents during the Gulf War, and other incidents have heightened awareness regarding the potential for terrorists acts involving what are now characterized as *weapons of mass destruction* (WMD).

A WMD incident in which chemical, biological, or radiological materials are used in conjunction with explosives or released environmentally under certain circumstances has the potential to cause significant numbers of casualties as well as creating widespread public panic. Such situations require a very different approach to ensure appropriate steps are taken to protect medical service providers and facilities against unnecessary exposure.

In any terrorist incident that produces mass casualties and extensive damage, the first consideration should be whether some chemical, biological or radiological agent was involved. The presence of a hazardous material with the accompanying prospect of contamination and exposure drastically alters the tactics that should be employed by law enforcement personnel.

Safety of Fire Fighters and EMS personnel through scene monitoring/sensors and protective equipment MUST be foremost in order to diminish the risk of serious illness, injury or death.

The key safety factor in a radiation incident is to minimize radiation exposure to Fire and EMS personnel. Minimizing radiation exposure is accomplished by *time*, *distance* and *shielding*.

Time means limiting the time that personnel are exposed to a radiation source. For example, personnel that are exposed for one hour receive four times the exposure that would be received in 15 minutes.

Distance means reducing the proximity to a radiation source. *Distance* is very effective because safety increases with the square of the distance. For example, if the distance to a radiation source is doubled, exposure decreases four times (a factor of four).

Shielding is the use of materials to block radiation. *Shielding* includes a protective suit, or structures. Alpha and Beta radiation is easily shielded. Unfortunately, Gamma radiation requires lead shielding that is seldom available on an emergency scene.

> **Critical Factor:** Radiation exposure to Fire and EMS personnel can be reduced by using the principles of time, distance, and shielding.

Emergency Medical Considerations

EMS personnel responding to an incident where radiation is involved or suspected must remember that the first priority remains the expedient delivery of appropriate emergency medical services to the patient, including transport to a hospital. The first consideration is to deal with the patient's medical condition first!

> **Critical Factor:** Treat a patient's medical condition first.

In a first responder situation, ambulance, rescue, or medical services personnel will not know whether the patient is contaminated or exposed unless:

1. They are advised in advance by the party requesting assistance
2. They are advised on arrival by other responders such as police or fire officials that radioactive materials are present at the scene
3. They are advised by the patient that he or she is contaminated or was exposed
4. They determine from their own observation of the accident site that contamination or exposure is a possibility, i.e., from visual signs, placards, or documents such as shipping papers.

Information regarding the source of the radiation, type of radioactive material involved, and length of time of exposure is valuable data that should be gathered at the scene if possible, but it does not alter the role of EMS personnel with respect to the handling and transport of the patient.

At the same time, it is important that EMS personnel remember the distinction between exposure and contamination. They should remember that there is little, if any, chance they will encounter a radiological incident that poses a serious threat to their own health and safety. While accidents involving small amounts of radioactive material may occur in industry or commerce at any time, incidents that involve high-level, dangerous amounts of radiation are extremely rare and almost never occur outside the surveillance of qualified experts (terrorism is the exception).

The patient that is exposed but not contaminated requires no special handling except what is appropriate to the illness or injury. Such a patient presents no radiological threat to medical personnel. The patient is not radioactive.

When contamination is known to be present, or suspected but unconfirmed, EMS personnel should take steps to minimize the spread of contamination to themselves and the transport vehicle.

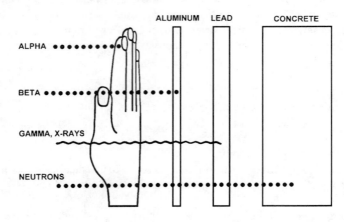

Radiation penetration and shielding

Industrial Sources of Radiation

LOCATIONS AND MATERIALS	RADIATION SOURCES	SOURCE STRENGTH	COMMENTS
Gauges, Sources, Static Eliminators.	Iridium-192, Cesium-137, Cobalt-60, Radium-226, Neutrons, Americium-241, Polonium-210.	Greater than about 4 TBq.	Sealed sources, and if leaking, presents surface contamination.
X-ray Machine Sterilizers, Processors, and Particle Accelerators.	X-rays, Protons, Deuterons, Electrons, Gammas, Cesium-137, Cobalt-60.	~4 TBq to ~40 PBq.	Anywhere in an industrial area. Be aware of possible activation products.
Mineral Extraction and Processing, including phosphate fertilizers, oil, natural gas, and coal.	Naturally occurring Radioactive Materials-Uranium, Thorium, and their progeny.	Generally low level with external exposures from background level to about 0.01 mSv (1 mrem).	Dispersed low level material and scale build-up in piping. Also, in gauges as noted above. Radon is a possible concern.
Power Sources.	Plutonium-238, Strontium-90.	Plutonium-238: Up to 4 GBq; Strontium-90: Up to 1 TBq.	In equipment in isolated areas.
Radioluminescent Materials.	Promethium-147, Tritium, Radium-226.	Up to tens of TBq.	Various applications, and if leaking, surface contamination.

Legend: TBq Tera Becquerel
GBq Giga Becquerel

Medical Sources of Radiation

LOCATIONS AND MATERIALS	RADIATION SOURCES	SOURCE STRENGTH	COMMENTS
Cancer Treatment Areas	Cobalt-60 and Cesium-137	~1 to 10 Gy over several hours at about 1 meter if the source is exposed.	Found in therapy rooms.
Sources and Applicators	Cesium-137, Iridium-192, Radium-226, Phosphorous-32, Strontium-90, Iodine-125.	Tens of MBq	Therapy and nuclear medicine areas.
Radiopharnaceuticals	Iodine-123, Phosphorous-32, Technetium-99m, Thalium-201	Tens of MBq	Storage, nuclear medicine areas, and transportation.
	Iodine-131, Strontium-89	Hundreds of MBq	
X-ray machines and Accelerators	X-rays and electrons.	~0.01 Gy per minute at the source	Radiology or therapy rooms.

Comparison of Weapons Effects by Yield in Kilometers

Weapon Effect	Weapon Yield (KT)					
	0.01 KT	0.1 KT	1 KT	10 KT	100 KT	1 MT
Blast: Lethality						
Threshold: 30 psi (30–50)	0.038	0.081	0.18	0.38	0.81	1.8
50%: 50 psi (50–75)	0.030	0.065	0.14	0.30	0.65	1.4
100%: 75 psi (75–115)	0.025	0.055	0.12	0.25	0.55	1.2
Blast: Lung Damage						
Threshold: 8 psi (8–15)	0.074	0.16	0.34	0.74	1.6	3.4
Severe: 20 psi (20–30)	0.046	0.098	0.21	0.46	0.98	2.1
Blast: Eardrum Rupture						
Threshold: 5 psi	0.096	0.21	0.44	0.96	2.1	4.4
50%: 14 psi	0.055	0.11	0.25	0.54	1.1	2.5
Thermal: Skin Burns						
50% First degree (2–3 cal/cm²)	0.13	0.37	1.2	3.4	8.3	17
50% Second degree (4–5 cal/cm²)	0.089	0.24	0.86	2.5	6.5	14
50% Third degree (6–8 cal/cm²)	0.073	0.18	0.71	2.1	5.6	12
Retinal burns (0.0001 cal/cm²)	10	20	33	49	66	84
Flash blindness (0.16 cal/cm²)	0.44	1.3	3.7	9	18	31
Ionizing Radiation Effects						
100% death, < 1 day: 10,000 cGy	0.14	0.21	0.36	0.66	1.1	1.9
100% death, few days: 1000 cGy	0.21	0.36	0.65	1.0	1.6	2.4
50% death, weeks: 450 cGy	0.25	0.45	0.77	1.2	1.7	2.6
< 5% deaths, years: 100 cGy	0.36	0.64	1.0	1.5	2.0	3.0
Start acute effects: 50 cGy	0.43	0.75	1.1	1.6	2.2	3.1

Relative Radiosensitivity of Various Tissues Based on Parenchymal Hypoplasia

Organs	Relative Radiosensitivity	Chief Mechanism of Parenchymal Hypoplasia
Lymphoid organs; bone marrow, testes and ovaries; small intestines; embryonic tissue	High	Destruction of parenchymal cells, especially the vegetative or differentiating cells
Skin; cornea and lens of eyes; gastrointestinal organs: cavity, esophagus, stomach, rectum	Fairly high	Destruction of vegetative and differentiating cells of the stratified epithelium
Growing cartilage; the vasculature; growing bones	Medium	Destruction of proliferating chondroblasts or osteoblasts; damage to the endothelium; destruction of connective tissue cells and chondroblasts or osteoblasts
Mature cartilage or bone; lungs; kidneys; liver; pancreas; adrenal gland; pituitary gland	Fairly low	Hypoplasia secondary damage to the fine vasculature and connective tissue elements
Muscle; brain; spinal cord	Low	Hypoplasia secondary damage to the fine vasculature and connective tissue elements, with little contribution by the direct effects on parenchymal tissues

Dose, Onset, and Duration of Symptoms

Dose (cGy)	Symptoms	Onset	Duration
0–35	None	N/A	N/A
35–75	Mild Nausea Headache	6 Hours	12 Hours
75–125	Nausea/ Vomiting (30%)	3–5 Hours	24 Hours
125–300	Nausea/Vomiting (70%)	2–3 Hours	3–4 Days
300–530	Nausea/Vomiting (90%)	2 Hours	3–4 Days
	Diarrhea (10%)	2–6 Hours	2–3 Weeks
530–830	Severe Nausea/Vomiting (90%)	1 Hour	Direct Transit into GI Syndrome
	Diarrhea (10%)	1–8 Hours	
830–3000	Severe Nausea/Vomiting (90%)	3–10 Min	Persists Until Death
	Disorientation (100%)	3–10 Min	30 Min–10 Hours

Medical Assay of the Radiological Patient

Test	Location/Facility			
	Decontamination Point	Medical Treatment Unit (Level 2)	Hospital (Level 3)	Tertiary Care (Level 4)
Nasal swabs for inhalation of contaminants	+			
External contamination	+		+	
Urine and stool sample for internal contamination		Baseline sample	24 hour sample	+
CBC/platelets	If practical	Baseline sample and then daily	Daily for 2 weeks	Daily for 2 weeks
Absolute Lymphocyte Count		Every 4–12 hours	Every 4–12 hours for 3 days	
Human Leukocyte Antigen (HLA) subtyping		Draw sample	Draw sample before lymphocyte count falls	Draw sample before lymphocyte count falls
Cytomegalovirus (CMV)			+	+
Hemoglobin Agglutinin			+	+
Human Syncytial Cell Virus Antibodies				+
Human Immunovirus			+	+
Vesiculovirus				+
Lymphocyte Cytogenetics		Draw sample	Draw sample before lymphocyte count falls	+

Note: + indicates test should be performed at this location/level of care.

Symptom-Oriented Therapy for the Cutaneous Radiation Syndrome

Symptom	Treatment	Application	Dosage	Result	Side Effects
Pruritus	Anti-histamines	Oral	As appropriate	Relief of itch	Sedation
Erythema	Steroids	Topical	2 X daily	Alleviation	None when used less than 3 weeks
Blisters	Steroids TCDO	Wet dressing	3 X daily	Alleviation	
Dryness	Linoleic acid cream	Topical	1 X daily	Inhibition of water loss	
Keratoses	Tretinoin Acitretin	Topical oral	1 X daily 0.1-0.3 mg/kg	Clearance moderate	Irritation; dryness of lips
Inflammation	Mometasone	Topical	3–4 X week	Alleviation	
Fibrosis	IFN gamma PTX and Vitamin E	Subcutaneous Oral	50 mg 3 X week 400 mg 3 X daily + 300 mg 1 X daily	Reduction Reduction	Fever

Blocking and diluting agents Blocking and diluting agents work by preventing the uptake of a radionuclide in a target organ or by overwhelming the organ with stable compounds that reduce the uptake and incorporation of the radionuclide into that target organ. Potassium iodide is an excellent example of a blocking agent, and must be given before or within 6 hours of exposure to radioiodine (see Table Below).

Table-Recommended Prophylactic Single Doses of Stable Iodine

Age Group	Mass of Total Iodine	Mass of KI	Mass of KIO_3	Volume of Lugols Solution
Adults/ adolescents (over 12 yr)	100 mg	130 mg	170 mg	0.8 ml
Children (3–12 yr)	50 mg	65 mg	85 mg	0.4 ml
Infants (1 mo to 3 yr)	25 mg	32.5 mg	42.5 mg	0.2 ml
Neonates (birth to 1 mo)	12.5 mg	16 mg	21 mg	0.1 ml

* KIO_3 potassium iodate

DOSE (estimate)	INITIAL SYMPTOMS	INITIAL SYMPTOMS INTERVAL ONSET–END	ANTIEMETIC PRETREATMENT EFFECT	MEDICAL PROBLEMS	INDICATED MEDICAL TREATMENT	DISPOSITION WITHOUT MEDICAL CARE	DISPOSITION WITH MEDICAL CARE	CLINICAL REMARKS
0–35 cGy	None	N/A	Dry mouth Headache	Anxiety	Reassurance. Counsel at redeployment	duty	duty	Potential for combat anxiety manifestation
35–75 cGy	Nausea, mild headache	ONSET 6 hrs END 12 hrs	Not determined	Anxiety	Reassurance. Counsel at redeployment	duty	duty	Mild lymphocyte depression within 24 hours
75–125 cGy	Transient mild nausea, vomiting in 5–30% of personnel	ONSET 3–5 hrs END 24 hrs	5–30% of personnel nauseated without emesis	Potential for delayed traumatic and surgical wound healing, minimal clinical effect	Debridement and primary closure of any and all wounds. No delayed surgery.	Restricted duty No further radiation exposure elective surgery or wounding	Restricted duty No further radiation exposure	Moderate drop in lymphocyte, platelet, and granulocyte counts. Increased susceptibility to opportunistic pathogens.
125–300 cGy	Transient mild to moderate nausea and weakness in 20–70% of personnel. Mild to moderate fatigability and weakness in 25–60% of personnel	ONSET 2–3 hrs END 2 days	Decreased vomiting Possible increase of fatigability	Significant medical care may be required at 3–5 wks for 10–50% of personnel. Anticipated problems should include infection, bleeding, and fever. Wounding or burns will geometrically increase morbidity and mortality	Fluid and electrolytes for GI losses Consider cytokines for immunocompromised patients (follow granulocyte counts)	LD_5 to LD_{10} Restricted duty No further radiation exposure, elective surgery or wounding. May require delayed evacuation from theater during nuclear war IAW command guidance.	Restricted duty No further radiation exposure, elective surgery or wounding	If there are more than 1.7×10^9 lymphocytes per liter 48 hrs after exposure, it is unlikely that an individual has received a fatal dose. Patients with low (300–500) or decreasing lymphocyte counts, or low granulocyte counts should be considered or cytokine therapy and biologic dosimetry using metaphase analysis where available

Source: US Department of the Army—Treatment of Nuclear and Radiological Casualties US Army Medical Department Center and School Fort Sam Houston, Texas 78234–6175

Chapter 6

Weapons of Mass Effect— Explosives

Introduction

Explosive devices are effective for three basic reasons:

1. They create mass casualties and property destruction. (In other words, a weapon of mass destruction (WMD)).
2. Explosives are a major psychological weapon. An explosion instills terror and fear in survivors and the unaffected population. (A weapon of mass effect (WME)).
3. Secondary explosive devices render a site unsecured, greatly complicating medical, rescue, and suppression efforts (WME).

> **Critical factor:** Explosives are very effective weapons for creating mass casualties and fear.

There is every indication that Fire/EMS personnel will witness an increase in explosive terrorism and tactical violence. The Internet abounds with information about simple explosives and simple timing devices that can be made at home. Commercial explosives are readily available and military explosives can be accessed in world black markets.

Explosive Physics

An explosive material is a substance that is capable of rapidly converting to a gas with an extreme increase in volume. This rapid increase in volume causes heat and noise, and a shock wave that travels outward from the detonation.

The most damaging by-product of an explosion is the shock wave. The shock wave is an energy wave that originates from the source and travels outward in all directions. The wave travels the course of least resistance. It reflects off hard objects such as strong walls or buildings and becomes concentrated in spaces such as hallways or areas between buildings.

The strength and characteristics of explosives are measured by the speed of the shock waves they produce. This is measured in feet per second (fps) or meters per second (mps). The dividing line between low explosives and high explosives is determined by their velocity of detonation. A more precise and scientific definition is that a low explosive is an explosive that deflagrates at less than the speed of sound into the remaining unreacted explosive material. A high explosive is an explosive that deflagrates faster than the speed of sound in the remaining explosive material. A low explosive may become a high explosive by the way it is contained or initiated. Black powder, when burned in an open area, will not detonate. If you confine the powder in a container such as a pipe bomb, the outcome is very different. The same applies with the initiation of high explosives. When C4 is ignited it will burn without detonating. If you introduce a shock to C4 via a blasting cap, you get an explosive detonation yield.

> **Critical factor:** Explosives produce a very high-speed, damaging shock wave.

Some explosives have a shock wave that produces a pushing effect. Detonation or deflagration that is slower than the speed of sound causes this push effect. Deflagration is a very rapid combustion that is less than the speed of sound. These explosives push obstacles and are commonly used for applications such as quarrying, strip mining or land clearing. Black powder, smokeless powder, and photoflash powders are examples of deflagrating or low explosives.

High explosives have a sharp shattering effect. This shattering effect is referred to as the explosives' brisance. High explosives are very brissant, and produce shock waves greater than the speed of sound. For example military explosives such as C4 produce a shock wave of twenty-four thousand f.p.s. High explosives (high brisance) have a very sharp and shattering effect. These explosives do extensive damage, causing severe injuries with a high percentage of fatalities.

An explosive shock wave creates another effect that is called blast over-pressure. Air in the vicinity of the explosion is compressed and expands creating a pressure higher than atmospheric pressure. Blast over-pressure causes barotrauma damage in the form of air embolisms and damages tethered organs. This pressure also causes severe structural damage to buildings.

Types of Explosives

Dynamite is a high explosive that generates a shock wave of fourteen to sixteen thousand fps. It is readily available and legally procured in states that issue a blaster's permit. Quantities are stored on construction sites and are frequently stolen. Dynamite is also used on farms for digging, land clearing and stump removal. Due to its availability, ease of use, stability, and explosive power, Dynamite is a popular choice for improvised explosive devices (IED's).

Black powder and smokeless powder are also popular IED explosives. They can be easily purchased in small quantities in gun shops that cater to ammunition reloading hobbyists. These explosives are frequently used in pipe bombs. Black powder is a deflagrating explosive that detonates with extreme force when stored in a confined container.

Ammonium nitrate is another common civilian explosive. Ammonium nitrate fertilizer when mixed with a catalyst will detonate with violent force. This explosive is frequently used in agricultural operations, and was the explosive that was used in the Oklahoma City bombing.

Military explosives are extremely powerful, even in small quantities. The most well known type is a plastic explosive called C4. It is soft and pliable, resembling a block of clay. C4 may be cut, shaped, packed and burned without detonating. When detonated, C4 explodes violently and produces a very high speed shock wave.

Similar plastic explosives are available on foreign markets. Other military explosives include Semtex, TNT, Tritonal, RDX, and PETN.

All explosives (civilian and military) require an initial high-impact and concentrated shock to cause detonation. A small explosive device called an initiator produces this initiating shock. Initiators are a key step in a chain of events called the explosive train. The most common type of initiator is a blasting cap.

The first step in the explosive train is a source of energy to explode the initiator. This source is usually electrical, but can be from thermal, mechanical, or a combination of the three sources. The initiator contains a small amount of sensitive explosive such as mercury fulminate. The detonation of the initiator produces a concentrated and intense shock that causes a high order detonation of the primary explosive. The explosive train is diagrammed as follows:

 Initiating energy = initiator explosion = main explosive detonation

Improvised Explosive Devices (IED)

An IED is any explosive device that is not a military weapon or commercially produced explosive device. In essence, IED's are homemade. It is important to realize that "homemade" devices can vary from being simple to highly sophisticated. Do not perceive IED's as being a high school product constructed from an Internet bomb recipe.

Approximately eighty to ninety percent of IED's are made from smokeless powder or Dynamite (Eglin Air Force Base, Florida, EOD School). Devices made from C4 or Semtex are rare, and usually lead investigators to suspect foreign sources.

Timers can be chemical, electrical, electronic, or mechanical. Simple timers include watches or alarm clocks that close an electrical circuit at a preset time. Electronic timers operate in a similar fashion, but are more reliable and precise. Some electronic timers or initiating devices can be activated from radio signals from a remote site. In most cases, timers cause electrical energy to be routed from batteries to an initiator (usually an electric blasting cap)

Other devices have no timer, and are designed to detonate when people or emergency responders in particular trigger the detonation. These devices are called booby traps. In simple devices, a trip wire or mechanical switch initiates the detonation. When the wire is touched or the device is tampered with, an explosion occurs. In more sophisticated devices, an invisible beam that is broken by people walking in front of the beam causes the detonation. Other high tech booby traps include light, sound, or infrared triggering systems.

> **Critical factor:** Improvised explosive devices vary in the type of explosive, form of initiation, and degree of sophistication.

Chemical, Nuclear and Biological IED's

An IED may be used to initiate a chemical, biological, or nuclear event. In these cases, the improvised explosive is used to scatter a chemical or biological pathogen or toxin.

A projected emerging phenomenon is the "dirty" weapon, an improvised nuclear device (IND) or a Radiological Dispersal Device (RDD). An IND/RDD does not involve a nuclear explosion like a military nuclear weapon. In an IND/RDD, conventional explosives are used to scatter radioactive materials.

Critical factor: Conventional explosives can be used to disperse chemical or radiological agents. Remember to assess the incident scene for radiological presence.

Secondary Devices

High threats to Fire/EMS responders are secondary devices. Secondary devices are timed devices or booby traps that are designed and placed to kill emergency responders. The objective is to create an emergency event such as a bombing or fire that generates an emergency response. The secondary device explodes and may cause more injuries than the original event.

Secondary devices can be used to create an entrapment situation. Beware of a situation that lures responders into narrow areas with only one escape route. A narrow dead-end alley is a classic example.

A key to surviving an entrapment situation is to recognize the scenario by surveying the overall scene. A narrow focus (called tunnel vision) obscures the big picture. **Look around!** Do not concentrate on a small portion of the incident scene. Look for trip wires, suspicious packages, and objects that appear to be out of place. Be especially aware of dumpsters or abandoned vehicles. Question civilians familiar with the area if possible. Try entry by an alternate route.

Critical factor: BEWARE OF SECONDARY DEVICES

Safety Precautions

1. Avoid radio transmissions within at least fifty feet of a suspected device. Electro magnetic radiation (EMR) from radio transmissions can trigger an electric blasting cap or cause a sophisticated device to detonate.
2. Avoid smoking within fifty feet (or further) from a suspicious device.
3. Do not move, strike, or jar a suspicious item. Do not look in a suspicious container or attempt to open packages.
4. Memorize a clear description of suspicious items.
5. Establish a hot zone for five hundred feet around small devices, and one thousand feet around large devices or vehicles. (Large zones may not be practical in congested downtown areas.) Maintain the required hot zone until bomb technicians advise otherwise.
6. Try to stay upwind from a device. Explosions create toxic gases.

7. Take advantage of available cover such as terrain, buildings, or vehicles. Remember that shock waves bounce off surrounding obstacles.

Basic Search Techniques

Fire fighters often conduct primary searches or assist bomb experts in conducting a thorough search for explosive devices. Remember that emergency responders are not trained to "clear" an area; only bomb technicians should perform this function.

> **Critical factor:** Bomb technicians are the only personnel qualified to "clear" an area or remove/disarm an explosive device.

In building searches, always search from the outside in. Building occupants are an excellent source of information, because they know what objects are supposed to be in a given location. Occupants can tell you that a trash basket has always been there, or that a paper bag is Joe's lunch. Likewise, they can point out the innocent looking newspaper machine was never there before. In building interiors, custodians can assist in unlocking areas and pointing out obscure storage areas.

Search from the floor to the ceiling. Often objects that are not at eye level are unseen. Adopt the habit of making a floor level sweep, followed by an eye level sweep, and finally a high wall and ceiling sweep.

Begin vehicle searches from the outside to the inside (just like buildings). If the driver is present, assign one person to distract the driver from observing advanced search techniques. Leave the trunk and doors closed, and concentrate on the outside. Avoid touching the vehicle; touching can activate motion switches. Never open the vehicle until trained technicians arrive.

Always emphasize the safety precautions previously discussed in this chapter. When in doubt, wait for bomb technicians. You can save lives by establishing a hot zone and exercising effective scene control.

Key safety steps in an unsecured area are:

★ Avoid radio transmissions or smoking within fifty feet of a suspected device.

★ Do not move, strike, or jar a suspicious item.

★ Establish a hot zone five hundred feet around a small device and one thousand feet around a large device or vehicle. (These distances may not be practical in urban areas.)

Refer to Quick References for additional information on Vehicle Bomb Explosion Hazard and Evacuation Tables from the ATF.

Chapter 7

Weapons of Mass Effect—Cyber-Terrorism

Introduction

In December 1998, The Department of Defense (DoD) announced that information warfare was being institutionalized as the new operational battlespace. The three traditional battlegrounds were land, sea, and air. These elements are now called "battlespaces" to incorporate the fourth element of information warfare. In essence, cyberspace is formally recognized as permeating all DoD battlespaces. Information operations are also a key law enforcement battlespace. Like DoD, law enforcement agencies are subject to cyber attack, and must protect this essential "battlespace" element.

Critical Infrastructure

The critical infrastructure consists of, in part, information management systems, telecommunications, dispatch centers, cable television, power production, water service, natural gas and their storage facilities, transportation and distribution mechanisms. Protecting this infrastructure against physical and electronic attack and ensuring the availability of the infrastructure is a complex issue. In 1998, it was estimated that computer intrusions cost corporations $236 million (Computer Security Institute).

The elements of the critical infrastructure that are most important to law enforcement are the essential systems in the public safety infrastructure. The general areas of this infrastructure are communications, NCIC, computer aided dispatch (CAD) systems, geo-based information systems (GIS), e-mail, and informational databases.

The most critical system is communications. The law enforcement dispatch system includes repeaters, consoles, enhanced trunking systems, transmitters, and receivers. All of these elements are electronic, and susceptible to data corruption. The public also has a communications system; namely, 911. All aspects of an enhanced 911 system are computer driven including electronic switching, automatic location identification, and automatic call routing. Most systems also have a database of caller medical information, hazardous materials data, or location descriptions.

There are many cases of hackers corrupting the telephone switching system for the purpose of making free toll calls. At a more serious level, 911 systems have been "hacked" for malicious purposes. The result has been missed calls and system outages.

Computer aided dispatch (CAD) systems include electronic mapping, system status software, automatic vehicle location software, and databases of call information. A failure of any of these systems results in downgrading dispatching to a manual mode. Calls are missed, unit locations erased, and call data lost during critical peak periods. Information operations sabotage during a terrorist incident could greatly inhibit the ability of the Fire/EMS delivery system to effectively respond.

Information Databases

Information databases and decision systems have progressed from an oddity to a necessity in less than a decade. Some of the information now routinely used includes:

> Criminal histories
> Electronic mapping
> Medical protocols
> Logistics data
> Disaster plans
> Personnel information
> Hazardous materials response guidelines
> Building pre-plans
> Financial reports and spreadsheets

A loss of information in any of the previous systems results in costly efficiency losses. More importantly, an intentional manipulation of data may go unnoticed for a significant duration, and result in poor decisions being made from inaccurate data.

Fire/EMS agencies, at all levels, must secure information systems and prepare for continuous infrastructure threats; having the will to do so is another matter entirely. Systems security is not a "do it once and you're done" proposition. An effective security plan is similar to an effective response plan. It must evolve, and develop as the threat to systems evolve and develop.

The Questioning of Computer Data

Data on a computer screen have a high degree of credibility. Anyone born after 1950 was raised in front of a television screen. Anyone born after 1970 was raised in front of a computer screen along with the television. As a result, data on a screen has a very high degree of believability.

The habit of accepting electronic data without question must change, especially during tactical operations. When data does not agree with reasonable expectations, the data must be questioned, and data corruption suspected. (In other words, the data must be "in the ballpark.") For example, a database of tactical plans that indicates procedures that appear inaccurate or unsafe should be compared with a printed source or another data system. In another case, if the CAD system suddenly indicates grossly inaccurate unit status, the information should be checked and corruption suspected. Any uses of electronic data by tactical decision-makers should observe the following guidelines:

1. Do not blindly trust data screens.
2. Evaluate tactical data for a "reality check."
3. Check other sources when data corruption is suspected.

In a terrorism/tactical violence event, consider the possibility of a coordinated information attack. Suspect intentional data manipulation when there is a mysterious communications failure. Maintain low-tech information sources (books and paper) as an alternative to vulnerable electronic information.

Data Theft

How easy is it to walk into your agency, remove disks stacked on a desk, and walk out? If the data is removed, altered, and discreetly returned, great damage may result. If backup disks are removed, followed by a system attack, provisions for storing the system may be lost. There are several steps that should be taken in any public or private agency to protect vital data from simple theft:

Office design—No one should be able to freely enter an office area; place a door between the entry lobby or data storage areas. Fire and EMS stations must be secured when units are out of quarters.

Entry control—anyone entering an office or data storage area should encounter a receptionist/secretary or security officer before proceeding.

ID badges—visitors and guests should sign in, and be issued a security badge; employees should wear identification badges; procedures should require that any person without a badge be questioned.

Information storage—stored data should be locked and never stored on a desktop or open area; critical backup data should be stored in a safe at an off-premise location. (This is good advice for fire and severe weather protection as well as theft.)

Information disposal—discarded disks should be destroyed; paper should be shredded to prevent "dumpster diving."

Electronic entry—sensitive areas should be controlled by electronic entry; systems should provide printouts of all names, dates, and times of entries.

Data Protection Standards

Most local government response agencies are merely end-users of electronic data. They lack the sophistication of federal government agencies and private organizations regarding protection of critical data. Standards and protocols are needed as follows:

Data storage procedures
Detection of running system attacks (real time)
System restoration (disaster recovery)
Physical security protocols
Training standards for information technology security specialists

In the future, Fire/EMS agencies may have standards and protocols on information operations that rival tactical procedures. Presently, no such standards exist. At best, there is an inadequate mix of guidelines borrowed from private industry and federal agencies.

Many Fire/EMS agencies knowingly release sensitive information through the Internet. Agency home pages include links to computer aided dispatch data screens, tactical response information, and links to communications centers that include real-time audio radio traffic. The motive is usually an attempt to generate positive public relations. Unfortunately, this type of information is very helpful to an adversary. Take another look at your organization's Internet links and home pages and remove information that may make your system or your officers/deputies vulnerable.

Information Security Management

In the future, the Director of Information Security Management (ISM) will be a new position in progressive Fire/EMS agencies. Physical security is commonplace; information security will be just as important.

Presently, information security is haphazard at best, and certainly not a prominent unit in Fire/EMS organizational charts. In most agencies, security is relegated to someone in the information services (IS) department that usually has many other duties. In the ideal model, information security should pervade the organization. This means an information security department managed by a professional ISM. This department must be high in the management hierarchy and operate by professional standards and protocols.

An effective ISM department should have the following goals:

1. Develop and maintain systems for real-time detection of running cyber attacks.
2. Conduct on-going educational awareness programs for all internal agencies.
3. Stay informed regarding national level research and development efforts.
4. Maintain the standards and best practices of the information technology industry.
5. Maintain an intelligence system for crisis information about cyber threats.
6. Conduct aggressive investigations on all incidents relating to system attacks or data disruption
7. Implement and maintain a back-up system.

Chapter 8

Mass Casualty Decontamination

Basic Principles of Decontamination

Decontamination is defined as the process of removing or neutralizing a hazard from the environment, property, or life form. The management and treatment of contaminated casualties will vary with the situation and nature of the contaminant. Quick, versatile, effective and large capacity decontamination is essential. Casualties must not be forced to wait at a central point for decontamination.

Fire departments and hazardous materials response teams define the two types of decontamination as *technical decon* and *medical* or *patient decon. Medical* or *patient decon* is the process of cleaning injured or exposed individuals. Fire and EMS departments are equipped and structured for rapid and effective decontamination. Many fire departments have developed procedures that use existing low-tech equipment to accomplish effective victim decon.

Stages of Decontamination

The process for decontamination of casualties involves three stages called *"gross"*, *"secondary"*, and *"definitive"* decontamination.

Gross decontamination

1. First, evacuate the casualties from the high-risk area. (With limited personnel available to conduct work in contaminated environment or *hotzone,* a method of triage needs to be established.) Then decon those who can self-evacuate or evacuate with minimal assistance to decon sites first and then start decontamination of those who will require more assistance.

2. Remove the exposed person's clothing. The removal and disposal of clothing is estimated to remove 70 to 80 percent of the contaminant; others estimate 90 to 95 percent.
3. Perform a one-minute quick head-to-toe rinse with water. Six gallons of water for one minute over twenty-two square inches of surface exposed (ANSI standard).

Secondary decontamination

1. Perform a quick full-body rinse with water.
2. Wash rapidly with a cleaning solution from head to toe. Plain water has been found to be effective because of ease and rapidity of application. With certain biological agents, the 5% sodium hypochlorite (Clorox) solution may require more than ten minutes of contact. This is not possible in a mass casualty incident requiring rapid decontamination.
3. Rinse with water from head to toe.

Definitive decontamination

1. Perform thorough head to toe wash until clean. Rinse thoroughly with water.
2. Dry victim and have them don clean clothes.

Methods of Initial Decontamination

Note: This section is for Fire/EMS overview and familiarization. Decon operations should be managed by certified EMS Level II and/or hazardous materials technicians. The primary function of non-EMS Level I or II during decon operations is patient evaluation and treatment after the patient is decontaminated.

1. Prevailing weather conditions (temperature, precipitation, etc.) These affect site selection, willingness of the individual to undress and the degree of decontamination required.
2. Wind direction
3. Ground slope, surface material and porosity (grass, gravel, asphalt, etc.)
4. Availability of water
5. Availability of power and lighting
6. Proximity of the incident
7. Containment of run-off water if necessary or feasible
8. Supplies including personnel protective equipment and industrial-strength garbage bags
9. Clearly marked entry and exit points with the exit upwind, away from the incident area

10. A staging area at the entry point for contaminated casualties. (This is a point where casualties can be further triaged and be given self-decontamination aids, such as spray bottles with 0.5% solution of sodium hypochlorite solution of Fullers' Earth.)
11. Access to triage and other medical aid upon exit if required
12. Protection of personnel from adverse weather
13. Privacy of personnel (This will be a media-intensive event)
14. Security and control from setting up of the site to final cleanup of the site.

Decontamination Triage

In a mass casualty event, decontamination of chemically exposed patients must be prioritized or triaged. The intent of this process is similar to the triaging of trauma patients in a conventional incident. The objective is to first decontaminate salvageable patients that are in immediate need of medical care. Patients that are dead, or unsalvageable, should not be immediately decontaminated. Patients that are ambulatory and non-symptomatic are the lowest decontamination priority. Again, the primary objective is to immediately decontaminate patients that are exposed, yet salvageable.

> **Critical Factor:** The principle of triage is to first decontaminate victims that are severely exposed, yet salvageable.

The U.S. Army Soldier and Biological Chemical Command (SBCCOM) published a guide called Guidelines for Mass Casualty Decontamination During a Terrorism Chemical Agent Incident (January 2000). The SBCCCOM guidelines suggest the following factors for assigning decontamination triage priorities:

⭐ Casualties closest to the point of release
⭐ Casualties reporting exposure to vapor or aerosol
⭐ Casualties with liquid deposition on clothing or skin
⭐ Casualties with serious medical signs/symptoms (shortness of breath, chest tightness, etc.)
⭐ Casualties with conventional injuries

Emergency response agencies must adopt a local protocol that should be based on the following issues:

1. What is the nature of the incident? Severe exposure to nerve agents with major symptoms usually result in death.

2. Are there high quantities of antidotes available? For example, nerve agents require very high doses of Atropine and Valium (for seizures). Most EMS systems do not carry mass casualty quantities of these drugs,

3. Are personnel available to move and treat mass numbers of non-ambulatory patients? A single non-ambulatory patient requires two to four responders.

4. Ambulatory patients that are symptomatic or have been severely exposed should be immediately decontaminated.

5. Ambulatory patients that are non-symptomatic should be moved to a treatment area for possible clothing removal and medical evaluation.

6. Non-ambulatory patients should be evaluated in place while further prioritization for decontamination occurs (SBCCOM).

7. Patients that are in respiratory arrest, grossly contaminated with a liquid nerve agent, have serious symptoms, or fail to respond to Atropine injections should be considered deceased or expected to die (expectant in military terminology).

In extreme cases, a patient in a hot zone may require immediate treatment prior to decontamination. Treatment usually consists of immediate antidote administration and airway maintenance. Clothing removal is the only expedient method of field decontamination, with decontamination by showering or flushing later if appropriate.

Hospital Decontamination Standards

The Joint Commission on Accreditation of Healthcare Organizations (JCAHO) requires hospitals to be prepared to respond to disasters including hazardous materials accidents. The majority of hospitals that have decontamination capability utilize existing indoor infrastructure and do not have the ability to expand to accommodate mass casualties. Outside the standard universal protection procedures followed by the medical community, required protective equipment and trained personnel are limited in the hospital system.

A hospital standard practice for hazmat response is to call the fire department. Due to the stress placed on the response system mitigating the effects of a large incident, hazmat teams will not be available. The hospitals will be placed at risk when the response system is stressed to the point that patients start self-referring or independent sources deliver patients to the hospital.

> **Critical Factor:** Hospitals are required by joint accreditation standards to have decontamination procedures and equipment.

The military has identified two types of decontamination: personnel and equipment. Personnel decontamination has been divided into two subcategories: hasty and deliberate. Specialized units within the military (U.S. Marine Corps Chemical Biological Incident Response Force and the National Guard's Civil Support Teams) have further subdivided deliberate decontamination to encompass ambulatory and non-ambulatory personnel.

Hasty decontamination is primarily focused on the self-decontaminating individual using the M258A1 skin decontamination kit. This kit is designed for chemical decontamination and consists of wipes containing a solution that neutralizes most nerve and blister agents. Another type of kit, the M291 decontamination kit, uses laminated fiber pads containing reactive resin, which neutralizes and removes the contaminant from a surface by mechanical and absorption methods. (These kits require user training, and are not usually available for civilian emergency response organizations.)

The procedure of removing and exchanging (donning and doffing) personnel protective clothing is also considered hasty decontamination. Deliberate decontamination is required when individuals are exposed to gross levels of contamination or for individuals who were not dressed in personnel protective clothing at time of contamination. The established process is to completely remove the individual's clothing, apply a decontamination solution (0.5% HTH) followed by a fresh water rinse, then use a chemical agent monitor (CAM) to detect the presence of nerve and blister agents or M-8 paper to validate the thoroughness of the decontamination process. At the end of this process the individual is provided new clothing and equipment. If the individual presents symptoms he or she will be processed through the heath care system.

Decontamination Site Set-up

The decontamination site should be established with the following consideration:

- ☆ Upwind from the source of contamination
- ☆ On a downhill slope or flat ground with provisions made for water run-off
- ☆ Water availability
- ☆ Decontamination equipment availability
- ☆ Individual supplies
- ☆ Health care facilities
- ☆ Site security

Mass Casualty Decontamination

Specialized military units have developed personnel decontamination sites that can process large numbers of contaminated personnel, both ambulatory and non-ambulatory. These systems or sites are capable (agent dependent) of processing up to 200 ambulatory or 35 non-ambulatory personnel per hour depending upon the agent(s) involved. The sites are set up in a tent that incorporates a shower system, which sprays a decontaminant followed by a rinse.

Step one of this process is removal of the patient's clothing. Ambulatory patients use a similar process that military personnel use during their doffing procedures. Non-ambulatory casualties' clothing is cut off by decon specialists.

Step two is to place clothing into disposable bins, which are sealed.

Step three is to remove personal effects, tag them, and place into plastic bags. Disposition of the personal effects will be determined later.

Step four is to apply a decontamination solution. For ambulatory casualties this is done through a shower system. Non-ambulatory casualties are sponged down.

Step five is for individuals to use brushes to clean themselves, or to be cleaned by a decon specialist. This step aids in the removal of the contaminant and allows for a three-minute contact time for the decontaminating solution.

Step six is a fresh water rinse.

Step seven is to monitor for the agent or contaminant. This is conducted using a CAM or M-8 paper for chemical agents or using a radiation meter for radiation.

Step eight is to don dry clothing.

Step nine is medical monitoring. Individual documentation is developed during this step.

Step ten individuals are released or transported to a medical facility.

The non-ambulatory site uses the same steps; however the casualty is moved along a series of rollers and cleaned by decon specialists. Care must also be taken at the non-ambulatory site to decontaminate the roller surface with a 5% percent solution HTH between patients. These sites are self-contained but require a water source and provide:

☆ Heated water (This is not required and may not be desired. Warm water opens the pores of the skin and could accelerate dermal exposure)

☆ Water run-off capture
☆ Decontamination solution
☆ Protection from the elements
☆ Privacy
☆ Medical monitoring during the decontamination process
☆ Post decontamination checks
☆ Clothing
☆ Site control

The specialized decontamination assets just described are from pre-positioned military units and not usually available for rapid response to civilian incidents. These units are highly competent and professional but limited by numbers and location. The military refers to them as low density, high demand assets. The U.S. Public Health Service has developed a similar capability resident in the Metropolitan Medical Response System Teams (MMRST) and the National Disaster Medical Response Teams (NMRT).

Radiation Decontamination

Radiation injuries per se do not imply that the casualty will present a hazard to the health care providers. Research has demonstrated that levels of intrinsic radiation present within the casualty from activation (after exposure to neutron and high-energy photon sources) are not life threatening. If monitoring for radiation is not available, decontamination for all casualties must be conducted. Removal of the casualty's clothing will reduce most of the contamination with a full body wash further reducing the contamination.

Wearing surgical attire or disposable garments such as Tyvek® will reduce the potential exposure of health care providers. Inhalation or ingestion of particles of radioactive material presents the greatest cross-contamination hazard. Care must be taken to capture run-off or retrieval of the material. Using industrial type vacuum cleaners commonly does this. The output air of these vacuum cleaners should be filtered with a HEPA filter to prevent re-release of the material into the air.

Decontamination Requirements for Various Agents

Decontamination requirements differ according to the type of chemical agent or material to which an individual or groups of individuals have been exposed. Regardless of reactivity and the potential chemicals that could be used in a mass casualty producing event, water is the accepted universal decontaminant.

The importance of early decontamination cannot be over emphasized with organophosphous compounds (nerve agents): due to the mechanism of action. Nerve agents may be absorbed through any surface of the body. Decontamination of the skin must be accomplished *quickly* if it is to be fully effective. Liquid agents may be removed by Fullers' Earth. Persistent nerve agents pose the greatest threat to health care providers. Once a patient has been decontaminated or the agent is fully absorbed, no further risk of contamination exists.

> **Critical Factor:** Early decontamination is critical for severe exposure to nerve agents.

Exposure to a vesicant (blister agent) is not always noticed immediately because of the latent effects. This may result in delayed decontamination or failure to decontaminate at all. Mucous membranes and eyes are too sensitive to be decontaminated with normal skin decontaminant solutions. Affected sensitive surfaces should be flushed with copious amounts of water or, if available, isotonic bicarbonate (1.26%) or saline (0.9%). Physical absorption, chemical inactivation and mechanical removal should decontaminate skin. Chemical inactivation using chlorination is effective against mustard, lewisite and ineffective against phosgene oxime. If water is used it must be used in copious amounts. If the vesicant is not fully removed the use of water will spread it.

> **Critical Factor:** Vesicant contamination may not be immediately noticed.

Choking agents will not remain in liquid form very long due to the extremely volatile physical property of choking agents. Decontamination is not required except when used in very cold climates. Choking agents are readily soluble in organic solvents and fatty oils. In water, choking agents rapidly hydrolyze into hydrochloric acid and carbon dioxide.

Blood agents will not remain in liquid form very long due to the extremely volatile physical property of blood agents. Decontamination is not required.

In the case of incapactants, total skin decontamination should be completed with soap and water at the earliest opportunity. Symptoms may appear as late as 36 hours after a percutaneous exposure, even if the individual is decontaminated within one hour of exposure.

Exposed personnel to riot control agents should be moved to fresh air, separated from other casualties, face into the wind with eyes open and breathe deeply.

Clothes should be removed and washed to preclude additional exposure from embedded residue.

Biological Agents

Biological agents are unique in their ability to inflict large numbers of casualties over a wide area by virtually untraceable means. The difficulty in detecting a biological agent's presence prior to an outbreak, its potential to selectively target humans, animals, or plants, and the difficulty protecting the population conspire to make management of casualties (including decontamination) or affected areas particularly difficult. The intrinsic features of biological agents that influence their potential use and establish management criteria include virulence, toxicity, pathogenicity, incubation period, transmissibility, lethality and stability.

If a dermal exposure is suspected it should be managed by decontamination at the earliest opportunity. Exposed areas should be cleansed using the appropriately diluted sodium hypochlorite solution (0.5%) or copious quantities of plain soap and water. The patient's clothing should also be removed as soon as possible.

Secondary contamination of medical personnel is a concern and can be avoided by strict adherence to universal medical precautions. Biological agents, for the most part, are highly susceptible to environmental conditions and all but a few present a persistent hazard.

Anthrax is a very stable agent; in a non-aerosolized state it presents only a dermal (requiring breaks or cuts in the skin) hazard. Weapons grade anthrax is very finely milled and presents a severe inhalation hazard. The strategy recommendations for potential exposure to anthrax are:

- ✶ Gather personal information from the potentially exposed individual(s)
- ✶ Explain the signs and symptoms of the disease
- ✶ Give them a point of contact to call if they show symptoms
- ✶ Send them home with the following instruction:
- ✶ Remove clothing and place it in a plastic bag, securing it with a tie or tape
- ✶ Shower and wash with soap for 15 minutes

The individuals should be informed of the lab analysis results of the suspected agent as soon as possible. If results are positive the individual the correct medical protocol will be administered.

Quick References

Biological Terrorism General Guidance Pocket Guide

Diagnosis: Be alert to the following

- ✷ Groups of individuals becoming ill around the same time
- ✷ Sudden increase of illness in previously healthy individuals
- ✷ Sudden increase in the following non-specific illnesses:
  - Pneumonia, flu-like illness, or fever with atypical features
  - Bleeding disorders
  - Unexplained rashes, and mucosal or dermal irritation
  - Neuromuscular illness
- ✷ Simultaneous disease outbreaks in human and animal populations
- ✷ Unusual temporal or geographic clustering of illness (for example, patients who attended the same public event, live in the same part of town, etc.)

Confirmation and technical support

- ✷ Alert local diagnostic laboratory
- ✷ To confirm cases, contact in-house or consulting infectious disease specialist
- ✷ Department of Justice Domestic Preparedness National Response Hotline (800-424-8802)
- ✷ If you need further help in clinical diagnosis call local health department and/or CDC
- ✷ Refer to the Army Handbook of Medical Management of Biological Casualties (http://www.nbc-med.org/others/)

Decontamination considerations

- ✷ Decontamination of patients usually not required for biological agents
- ✷ Clothing removal & biosafety bagging is recommended
- ✷ Handle equipment used according to standard infection control practices (see infection control practitioner or APIC website at www.APIC.org)

74

Institutional reporting

★ If reasonable suspicion of biological warfare agent exposure, contact hospital leadership (Chief of Staff, Hospital Director, etc)

★ Immediately discuss hospital emergency planning implications

Public Health Reporting

★ Contact local public health office

★ If unable to reach local public health officer, contact CDC: 770-488-7100

★ If needed, contact the FBI (for location of nearest office, see http://www.fbi.gov/contact/fo/info.htm)

Some Potential Biological Warfare Agents

Disease	Incubation	Symptoms	Signs	Diagnostic tests	Transmission and Precautions	Treatment (Adult dosage)	Prophylaxis
Inhaled Anthrax	1-6 days Range: 1 day to 8 weeks	Flu-like symptoms Respiratory distress (*Cutaneous Anthrax: Initial itching papule, then 1-3 cm painless ulcer, then necrotic center; fever)	Widened mediastinum on chest X-ray (from adenopathy) Atypical pneumonia Flu-like illness followed by abrupt onset of respiratory failure	Gram stain ("boxcar" shape) Gram positive bacilli in blood culture ELISA for toxin antibodies to help confirm	Aerosol inhalation *No person-to-person transmission* Standard precautions	Mechanical ventilation Antibiotic therapy Ciprofloxacin 400 mg iv q 8-12 h Doxycycline 200 mg iv initial, then 100 mg iv q 8-12 h Penicillin 2 mil units iv q 2 h – possibly add gentamicin	Ciprofloxacin 500 mg or Doxycycline 100 mg po q 12 h – 8 weeks (shorter with anthrax vaccine) Amoxicillin in pregnancy and children Vaccine if available
Botulism	12-72 hours Range: 2 hrs – 8 days	Difficulty swallowing or speaking (symmetrical cranial neuropathies) Symmetric descending weakness Respiratory dysfunction No sensory dysfunction No fever	Dilated or un-reactive pupils Drooping eyelids (ptosis) Double vision (diplopia) Slurred speech (dysarthria) Descending flaccid paralysis Intact mental state	Mouse bioassay in public health laboratories (5 – 7 days to conduct) ELISA for toxin	Aerosol inhalation Food ingestion *No person-to-person transmission* Standard precautions	Mechanical ventilation Parenteral nutrition Trivalent botulinum antitoxin available from State Health Departments and CDC	Experimental vaccine has been used in laboratory workers
Plague	1-3 days by inhalation	Sudden onset of fever, chills, headache, myalgia **Pneumonic:** cough, chest pain, hemoptysis **Bubonic:** painful lymph nodes	**Pneumonic:** Hemoptysis; radiographic pneumonia -- patchy, cavities, confluent consolidation **Bubonic:** typically painful, enlarged lymph nodes in groin, axilla, and neck	Gram negative coccobacilli and bacilli in sputum, blood, CSF, or bubo aspirates (bipolar, closed "safety pin" shape on Wright, Wayson's stains) ELISA, DFA, PCR	*Person-to-person transmission in pneumonic forms* Droplet precautions until patient treated for at least three days	Streptomycin 30 mg/kg/day in two divided doses x 10 days Gentamicin 1-1.75 mg/kg iv/im q 8 h Tetracycline 2-4 g per day	Asymptomatic contacts or potentially exposed Doxycycline 100 mg po q 12 h Ciprofloxacin 500 mg po q 12 h Tetracycline 250 mg po q 6 h all x 7 days Vaccine production discontinued
Tularemia "pneumonic"	2-5 days Range: 1-21 days	Fever, cough, chest tightness, pleuritic pain Hemoptysis rare	Community-acquired, atypical pneumonia Radiographic: bilateral patchy pneumonia with hilar adenopathy (pleural effusions like TB) Diffuse, varied skin rash May be rapidly fatal	Gram negative bacilli in blood culture on BYCE (Legionella) cysteine- or S-H-enhanced media Serologic testing to confirm: ELISA, microhemagglutination DFA for sputum or local discharge	Inhalation of agents *No person-to-person transmission but laboratory personnel at risk* Standard precautions	Streptomycin 30 mg/kg/day IM divided q 12 h for 10-14 days Gentamicin 3-5 mg/kg/day iv in equal divided shoulders x 10-14 days Ciprofloxacin possibly effective 400 mg iv q 12 h (change to po after clinical improvement) x 10-14 days	Ciprofloxacin 500 mg po q 12 h Doxycycline 100 mg po q 12 h Tetracycline 250 mg po q 6 h All x 2 wks Experimental live vaccine
Smallpox	12-14 days Range:7-17 days	High fever and myalgia; itching; abdominal pain; delirium Rash on face, extremities, hands, feet; confused with chickenpox which has less uniform rash	Maculopapular then vesicular rash -- first on extremities (face, arms, palms, soles, oral mucosa) Rash is synchronous on various segments of the body	Electron microscopy of pustule content PCR Public health lab for confirmation	*Person-to-person transmission* Airborne precautions Negative pressure Clothing and surface decontamination	Supportive care Vaccinate care givers	Vaccination (vaccine available from CDC)

The information in this card is not meant to be complete but to be a quick guide; please consult other references and expert opinion, and check drug dosages, particularly for pregnancy and children.

October 2001
VA access card:http://www.oqp.med.va.gov/cpg/cpg.htm
DoD access card:http://www.cs.amedd.army.mil/qmo
Produced by the Employee Education System for the Office of
Public Health and Environmental Hazards,Department of Veterans Affairs.

Sample BW Advisory to Emergency Services

Biological Agents

Recent events, and the ensuing extensive media coverage, have caused significant public interest in anthrax. This increased interest has prompted many people to contact local agencies for information and assistance. This document will provide: (1) information about biological agents, including anthrax; (2) suggestions for investigative inquiries, and (3) instructions for obtaining assistance when a threat is deemed credible.

Anthrax Information

The following information, obtained mostly from the Centers for Disease Control and Prevention, might prove helpful to those who have inquiries regarding anthrax:

- ✯ Anthrax is an infectious disease caused by the bacterium *Bacillus anthracis*. Anthrax is capable of forming spores, which can survive in the environment for long periods of time. Anthrax most commonly occurs in hoofed mammals, but can also infect humans.
- ✯ Inhalational anthrax (caused by breathing in the spores), cutaneous anthrax (caused by contact with an open wound), and gastrointestinal anthrax (caused by ingesting spores or bacteria) are NOT spread from person to person. Even if a person develops symptoms of inhalation anthrax or gastrointestinal anthrax, the person is NOT contagious to others regardless of whether or not the person is taking antibiotics.
- ✯ Initial symptoms of inhalation anthrax may resemble a common cold or the flu. It should be noted the country is currently entering the flu season. Flu-like symptoms are more likely indicators of usual seasonal illnesses rather than anthrax infection.
- ✯ If a person is exposed to anthrax, infection may be prevented with a wide range of antibiotic treatment.
- ✯ Vaccination is not recommended and the vaccine is not available to health care providers or the general public.
- ✯ Direct person-to-person contact spread of anthrax is extremely unlikely, if it occurs at all. Therefore, there is **no** need to immunize or treat contacts of persons ill with anthrax, such as household contacts, friends, or co-workers, unless they also were exposed to the same source of infection.
- ✯ Transforming anthrax into a weapon is an extremely difficult technological task.

Additional information regarding anthrax can be obtained by visiting the Center for Disease Control and Prevention website at **www.bt.cdc.gov**

Complaint Assessment

If an individual calls to report a suspicious incident related to possible anthrax exposure, the following questions can assist in assessing the credibility of the report.

★ Has there been a recent exposure to any suspicious foreign substance? If so, get a thorough description of the substance. Weaponized anthrax will be visible as a powder and is generally an off-white to yellowish tan powder, similar in texture to talcum powder.

★ Has there been a recent onset of flu-like symptoms? If so, how long have the symptoms lasted? Note that anthrax symptoms tend to be very severe and death generally occurs within three to four days.

★ Has there been recent receipt of suspicious letters or packages? Factors to consider include the following: (a) handwritten letters from an unknown source which have a postmark and no return address (many legitimate junk mail letters appear to be handwritten but use presorted stamps with no postmark); (b) letters or packages which contain an off-white to yellowish tan fine powder; (c) letters which contain an explicit threat.

Protocol for Credible Threats

If an investigator determines, based upon the above criteria, that the complaint is a credible suspicious incident related to anthrax, the complainant should be advised to do the following, when applicable:

★ Wash your hands with soap and warm water for 30 to 60 seconds, then wash your face. Also blow and wipe the nose.

★ Minimize handling the letter or package. If possible, place into plastic, such as a ziploc bag or plastic sheet protector. Anthrax does not produce a vapor or gas, and it cannot cause infection unless it gets into a cut or unless a sufficient amount is inhaled.

★ Close doors and windows in the room where the letter or package is located. Turn off air conditioning, heating, and fans to prevent the substance from circulating.

★ Contact a physician if symptomatic of flu.

If either of the following two conditions are present, immediately contact the local Law Enforcement, Public Health Authority and the FBI Field Office:

1. A letter or package containing an articulated threat of anthrax infection, whether or not a foreign substance is present.
2. A letter or package containing an off-white or yellowish tan powder.

There is no need to contact the FBI in the event of a suspicious letter or package that does not meet the above criteria.

When the FBI receives a complaint that meets one or both of the above criteria, an independent assessment will be conducted and further actions will be taken as necessary. The suspicious package should be handled using the following guidelines:

✴ Wear disposable latex or plastic gloves.
✴ Place the envelope inside another, larger envelope. A zip-lock plastic bag is preferred, but a manila envelope is sufficient. Do not shake or empty the envelope.

Note: See also the Biological Agent Questionnaire.

Biological Agent Questionnaire

VICTIM

1. Obtain the name, date of birth, address, and telephone number of victim.
2. Is the envelope at a residence or business? If it is a business, obtain business name, address, and type of business.
3. What is the occupation/employment of the victim? What are the victim's duties?
4. Has the victim received threats by mail or telephone before? If yes, give details.
5. Why does the victim think that he/she would be targeted?

ENVELOPE

1. Who or what is listed as the addressee on the envelope?
2. Who or what is listed as the return address on the envelope? Is the victim familiar with the sender?
3. Is the envelope typewritten or handwritten?
4. Does the envelope have a postmark? Where?
5. Does the envelope have a stamp? What kind of stamp? How many? Is there a meter strip?
6. What kind of the envelope (business, personal, etc.)?
7. How was the envelope sealed (tape, adhesive, etc.)?
8. Are there any additional markings on the exterior of letter?
9. Are there any stains on the exterior of the letter? Describe.

LETTER
1. Obtain summary of content of letter.
2. Is there an overt threat contained within the letter? Provide exact wording.
3. Are there any stains visible on the letter?

FOREIGN MATERIAL WITHIN THE ENVELOPE

1. Describe material found within envelope
2. Solid material:
   What is the color of the material?
   Describe granule size and shape (e.g. similar to sugar or powder)
   Does the material have an obvious odor? Do not purposely inhale the product.
   Did the material appear to become airborne upon opening?
3. Liquid:
   Describe the container size, type, and material (e.g. glass or plastic).
   What is the color of liquid?
   Is the liquid transparent or opaque?
   Is the liquid leaking from the container?

EXPOSURE

1. When was the envelope received (date and time)?
2. What was the mode of delivery (USPS, FedEx, etc.)?
3. Where are the envelope and letter currently?
4. What areas of the body were exposed to the material?
5. Was there a spill? If so, how large?
6. How many others had contact with the envelope or product?

HEALTH

1. Is the victim experiencing any physical symptoms? What are the symptoms?
2. How long after exposure did the symptoms occur?
3. Has the victim already seen a doctor? If yes, obtain the name and contact information for doctor.

NOTIFICATIONS

☆ Has the victim notified the local police, fire department, hazardous material team, or any other authority?

Bio Incident Threat Response

Biological Threat Agent Incidents

General incident objectives for responding to known or unknown potential biological threats.

Incident Objectives

★ Remove people from harm's way
★ Assess situation
★ Be cognizant of secondary devices
★ Secure the perimeter, set up operation areas, and establish hazard control zones (i.e., hot, warm and cold zone)
★ Control and identify agents involved
★ Rescue, consider decontamination, triage, treat and transport victims
★ Stabilize incident
★ Avoid additional contamination
★ Secure evidence and treat as a crime scene

On-Scene General Assessment

In assessing the situation commanders should consider:

★ Evacuating persons from the potential at-risk areas to minimize potential exposure
★ Number of apparent victims
★ Weather conditions, wind direction, atmospheric conditions, and time of day
★ Plume direction (vapor/cloud movement)
★ Types of injuries and symptoms presented (potentially none if a recent biological incident)
★ Information from witnesses (what they saw and heard)
★ Exact location of incident (type of occupancy)
★ Nature of agent and type of exposure
★ A safe access route and staging area
★ Isolating area and deny entry

Additionally commanders should insure first responders:

(AWARE)

★ **A**pproach scene from upwind/upgrade
★ **W**ear at least respiratory protection immediately
★ **A**lert other first responders of potentially dangerous conditions
★ **R**estrict entry to area
★ **E**valuate victims signs/symptoms and alert others

Observe possible indicators of a Biological Threat Agent:

★ Unusual Dead or Dying Animals
  • sick or dying animals, marine life, or people (note: this condition would not occur in the early stages of an incident)
★ Unusual Casualties
★ Unusual Liquid, Spray, Powder or Vapor
  • spraying and suspicious devices or packages

Hazard Assessment

Types:
★ Bacteria (e.g., anthrax, plague)
★ Virus (e.g., smallpox, viral hemorrhagic fevers)
★ Toxins (e.g., ricin, botulism)

Bacteria and Virus types are living organisms. They:
  • enter the body via inhalation, ingestion, or breaks in skin.
  • grow and reproduce.
  • can be contagious and cause an epidemic.

Toxins are not living organisms. They:
  • enter the body the same as pathogens.
  • are not contagious.

Characteristics:
★ Requires a dispersion device typically for aerosol generation
★ Non-volatile
★ Is not absorbed through intact skin
★ More toxic by weight than chemicals agents and industrial chemicals
★ Poses a possible inhalation hazard
★ Have a delayed effect ranging from several hours, to days, or weeks
★ Are invisible to our senses

Chemical Terrorism General Guidance Pocket Guide

Diagnosis: Be alert to following

★ Groups of individuals becoming ill around the same time

★ Any sudden increase in illness in previously healthy individuals

★ Any sudden increase in the following non-specific syndromes
  • Sudden unexplained weakness in previously healthy individuals
  • Hypersecretion syndromes (like drooling, tearing, and diarrhea)
  • Inhalation syndromes (eye, nose, throat, chest irritation; shortness of breath)
  • Skin-burn-like skin syndromes (redness, blistering, itching, sloughing)

★ Unusual temporal or geographic clustering of illness (for example, patients who attended the same public event, live in the same part of town, etc.).

Understanding exposure

★ Exposure may occur from vapor or liquid droplets and less likely contamination of food or water

★ Chemical effects are dependent on:
  • volatility and amount of a chemical, which influence exposure
  • water solubility (higher solubility leads to more mucosal and less deep lung deposition and toxicity)
  • increased fat solubility and smaller molecular size increase skin absorption

Confirmation of cases

★ Contact your local poison control center

★ Contact your local industrial hygienist or safety officer

★ Department of Justice (DOJ) Domestic Preparedness National Response Hotline (800-424-8802)

★ If you need further help in clinical diagnosis, call DOJ Chembio Help Line (800-368-6498)
★ Review US Army Chemical Casualty Care handbook (http://ccc.apgea.army.mil)

Decontamination considerations

★ Chemical warfare agents usually require removal of clothing and decontamination of the patient with soap and water.
★ Treating contaminated patients in the emergency department before decontamination may contaminate the facility.

Institutional reporting

★ If reasonable suspicion of chemical attack, contact your hospital leadership (Chief of Staff, Hospital Director, etc.).
★ Immediately discuss hospital emergency planning implications.

Public Health Reporting

★ Contact your local public health office (city, county, or state).
★ If needed, contact the FBI (for location of nearest office, see http://www.fbi.gov/contact/fo/info.htm).

Chemical Terrorism Agents and Syndromes (including Biologic Toxins)

Agents	Onset of symptoms	Symptoms	Signs	Clinical Diagnostic Tests	Decontamination	Exposure route and treatment (adult dosages)	Differential diagnostic considerations
Nerve agents	Vapor: seconds; Liquid: minutes to hours	**Moderate exposure:** Diffuse muscle cramping, runny nose, difficulty breathing, eye pain, dimming of vision, sweating; **High exposure:** The above plus sudden loss of consciousness, flaccid paralysis, seizures	Pinpoint pupils (miosis); Hyper-salivation; Diarrhea; Seizures	Red blood cell or serum cholinesterase (whole blood); **Treat for signs and symptoms; lab tests only for later confirmation** and dose estimation	Rapid disrobing; Water wash with soap and shampoo	**Inhalation & dermal absorption:** Atropine (2mg) iv or im (titrate to effect up to 6 to 15 mg); 2-PAMCl 600mg injection or 1.0 g infusion over 20-30 minutes; Additional doses of atropine and Diazepam or lorazepam to prevent seizures if >4 mg atropine given; Ventilation support	Pesticide poisoning from organophosphorous agents and carbamates cause virtually identical syndromes
Cyanide	Seconds to minutes	**Moderate exposure:** Dizziness, nausea, headache, eye irritation; **High exposure:** Loss of consciousness	**Moderate exposure:** non-specific findings; **High exposure:** convulsions, cessation of respiration	Cyanide (blood) or thiocyanate (blood or urine) levels in lab; **Treat for signs and symptoms; lab tests only for later confirmation**	Clothing removal	**Inhalation & dermal absorption:** Oxygen (face mask); Amyl nitrite; Sodium nitrite (300mg IV) and sodium thiosulfate (12.5g IV)	Similar CNS illness results from: Carbon monoxide (from gas or diesel engine exhaust fumes in closed spaces); H_2S (sewer, waste, industrial sources)
Blister Agents	2-48 hours	Burning, itching, or red skin; Mucosal irritation (prominent tearing, and burning and redness of eyes); Shortness of breath; Nausea and vomiting	Skin erythema; Blistering; Upper airways sloughing; Pulmonary edema; Diffuse metabolic failure	Often smell of garlic, horseradish, and mustard on body; Oily droplets on skin from ambient sources; No specific diagnostic tests	Clothing removal; Large amounts of water	**Inhalation &, dermal absorption:** Thermal burn type treatment; Supportive care; For Lewisite and Lewisite/Mustard mixtures: British Anti-Lewisite (BAL or Dimercaprol)	Diffuse skin exposure with irritants, such as caustics, sodium hydroxides, ammonia, etc., may cause similar syndromes. Sodium hydroxide (NaOH) from trucking accidents
Pulmonary agents (phosgene etc.)	1 - 24 (rarely up to 72) hours	Shortness of breath; Chest tightness; Wheezing; Mucosal and dermal irritation and redness	Pulmonary edema with some mucosal irritation (more water solubility = more mucosal irritation)	No tests available but source assessment may help identify exposure characteristics (majority of trucking incidents generating exposures to humans have labels on vehicle)	None usually needed	**Inhalation:** Supportive care; Specific treatment depends on agents	Inhalation exposures are the single most common form of industrial agent exposure (eg: HCl, Cl_2, NH_3). Mucosal irritation, airways reactions, and deep lung effects depend on the specific agent, especially water-solubility
Ricin (castor bean toxin)	18 -24 hours	**Ingestion:** Nausea, diarrhea, vomiting, fever, abdominal pain; **Inhalation:** chest tightness, coughing, weakness, nausea, fever	Clusters of acute lung or GI injury; circulatory collapse and shock	ELISA (from commercial laboratories) using respiratory secretions, serum, and direct tissue	Clothing removal; Water rinse	**Inhalation & Ingestion:** Supportive care; For ingestion: charcoal lavage	Tularemia, plague, and Q fever may cause similar syndromes, as may CW agents such as Staphylococcal enterotoxin B and phosgene
T-2 mycotoxin	2-4 hours	Dermal & mucosal irritation; blistering, necrosis; Blurred vision, eye irritation; Nausea, vomiting, and diarrhea; Ataxia; Coughing and dyspnea	Mucosal erythema and hemorrhage; Red skin, blistering; Tearing, salivation; Pulmonary edema; Seizures and coma	ELISA from commercial laboratories; Gas chromatography/Mass spectroscopy in specialized laboratories	Clothing removal; Water rinse	**Inhalation & dermal contact:** Supportive care; For ingestion: charcoal lavage; Possibly high dose steroids	Pulmonary toxins (O_3, NO_2, phosgene, NH_3) may cause similar syndromes though with less mucosal irritation.

The information in this card is not meant to be complete but to be a quick guide; please consult other references and expert opinion, and check drug dosages, particularly for pregnancy and children.

October 2001

VA access card:http://www.oqp.med.va.gov/cpg/cpg.htm

DoD access card:http://www.cs.amedd.army.mil/qmo

Produced by the Employee Education System for the Office of Public Health and Environmental Hazards, Department of Veterans Affairs.

Chemical Incident Threat Response

Chemical Threat Agent Incidents

General incident objectives for responding to known or unknown potential chemical threats.

Incident Objectives

☆ Remove people from harm's way

☆ Assess situation

☆ Be cognizant of secondary devices

☆ Secure the perimeter, set up operation areas, establish hazard control zones (i.e., hot, warm and cold zone)

☆ Control and identify agents involved

☆ Rescue, consider decontamination, triage, treat and transport victims

☆ Stabilize incident

☆ Avoid additional contamination

☆ Secure evidence and treat as a crime scene

On-Scene General Assessment

In assessing the situation commanders should consider:

☆ Evacuating persons from the potential at-risk areas to minimize potential exposure

☆ Weather conditions, wind direction, atmospheric conditions and time of day

☆ Plume direction (vapor/cloud movement)

☆ Number of apparent victims

☆ Types of injuries and symptoms presented

☆ Type of exposure and nature of possible agent

☆ Information from witnesses (what they saw and heard)

☆ Exact location of incident (type of occupancy)

☆ Suggested safe access route and staging area

☆ Isolate area and deny entry

Additionally commanders should ensure first responders:

(AWARE)

- ✻ **A**pproach scene from upwind/upgrade
- ✻ **W**ear at least respiratory protection immediately
- ✻ **A**lert other first responders of potentially dangerous conditions
- ✻ **R**estrict entry to area
- ✻ **E**valuate victims signs/symptoms and alert others

Observe possible indicators of a Chemical Threat Agent:

- ✻ Unusual or Dying Animals
  - lack of insects
- ✻ Unexplained Casualties
  - multiple victims
  - serious illness
  - nausea, trouble breathing
  - convulsions
  - definite casualty patterns
- ✻ Unusual Liquid, Spray or Vapor
  - droplets, oily film
  - unexplained odors
  - low clouds/fog unrelated to weather
- ✻ Suspicious Devices/Packages
  - unusual metal debris
  - abandoned spray devices
  - unexplained munitions

Hazard Assessment

Characteristics

- ✻ Requires a dispersion device typically for aerosol generation.
- ✻ Requires weaponization.
- ✻ Can be found as a solid, liquid or gas.
- ✻ The less volatile the agent the more persistent.
- ✻ Clinical effects vary from immediate to hours.

☆ Effects of chemical threat agents are affected by:
- temperature
- humidity
- precipitation
- wind speed
- nature of terrain and buildings

Types

☆ Nerve Agents
☆ Blister Agents
☆ Blood Agents
☆ Choking Agents
☆ Irritating Agents

The five classes of chemical threat agents all may produce incapacitation, serious injury, and/or death. Dose dependent in each victim. Effects range from mild to deadly.

NERVE AGENT ANTIDOTE DOSAGE
CHEMICAL WARFARE AGENT EXPOSURE

This information is regarding dosage considerations of exposure to chemical warfare agents at the Pine Bluff Arsenal. It should be noted, the suggested dosage may differ from those used in cases involving standard organophosphate poisoning.

ATROPINE

	DOSAGE (maximum SINGLE dose)
ADULT	2-6mg
ADOLESCENT ≥11YEARS	2mg
CHILD 2 thru 10 years	1 – 2 mg
INFANT <2 YEARS	0.5 – 1mg
ELDERLY (frail or medically compromised)	1mg

- In cases of progressive airway compromise, 2mg Atropine by auto-injector may be given to infants and elderly patients.

- IV atropine for treating systemic effects should be avoided in hypoxemic patients due to potential ventricular fibrillation.

- Do not use pupil size or heart rate as indications for atropine administration.

PRALIDOXIME (Protopam®, Protopam Chloride, 2-PAM Cl)

	DOSAGE
ADULT	• 600-1800mg IM injection by auto-injector or syringe 600mg may be repeated hourly for two times (qhx2) **OR** • 1g in 250ml NS or D₅W over 20-30 minutes (14.2mg/kg) repeated hourly for maximum of 3 doses
ADOLESCENT/CHILD >22 kg (50 pounds) (age 7 years to 16 years)	• 600-1800mg IM injection by auto-injector or syringe 600mg may be repeated hourly for two times (qhx2) **OR** • 15mg/kg in 250ml NS over 20-30 minutes repeated hourly for maximum of 3 doses
SMALL CHILD/INFANT ≤22 kg (50 pounds) (< 6 years)	• 150mg IM repeated hourly for two times (qhx2) **OR** • 15mg/kg in 250ml NS over 20-30 minutes repeated hourly for a maximum of 3 doses

Suggested Reconstitution: 3.3ml sterile water injected into 1g vial desiccated 2-PAM Cl shaken well yields 300mg/ml of 2-PAM Cl

- Hypertension, induced by high doses (greater than 15mg/kg) of Pralidoxime may be counteract with Phentolamine as follows:
  Adult: 5mg slow IV push   Child: 1mg slow IV push

DIAZEPAM (in prolonged seizure cases)

Adult	2-5mg IV OR 10mg IM repeated as needed
Child >5 years	1mg repeated at 2-5 minutes (max cumulative dose is 10mg)
Infant >30 days to Child age 5	0.2-0.5mg/kg repeated at 2-5 minutes (max cumulative dose is 5mg)

- Diazepam should be used in cases of prolonged seizures and in conscious/unconscious, severely intoxicated GB or VX cases.

ADH-EM [Parette] (Antidote Dosage) 5/1/00 REVISED 7-13-00

NERVE AGENT ANTIDOTE ADMINISTRATION PROTOCOL

Developed by Arkansas Department of Health — Chemical Stockpile Emergency Preparedness Program

Suggested Protocol for Symptomatic Treatment of Exposure to GB or VX — See Blister Agent Protocol for Exposure to Mustard

EXPOSURE	SIGNS & SYMPTOMS might include the following:	ADULT	ADOLESCENT (>35kg [77lb] apx.)	CHILD 7 thru 10 years (apx. 22 to 35kg [50-77lb])	SMALL CHILD 2 thru 6 years (apx. 11 to 22kg [25-50 lb])	INFANT <2 years (<11kg [25lb] apx.)
Minimal Vapor	• miosis • rhinorrhea	• observe • consider anticholinergic eye ointment/drops	• Observe • consider anticholinergic eye ointment/drops	• observe • consider anticholinergic eye ointment/drops	• observe • consider anticholinergic eye ointment/drops	• observe • consider anticholinergic eye ointment/drops
Mild Vapor	Those of Minimal Vapor & • dim &/or blurred vision • chest tightness • upper airway secretions	• Atropine 2mg IM or IV or 1 auto-inj. q5-10 min qs • 2-PAMCl consider 600mg IM or 1 auto-injector qh (max 3 doses)	• Atropine 2mg IM or 1 auto-inj. q5-10 min qs • 2-PAMCl consider 600mg IM or 1 auto-injector qh (max 3 doses) or • 1g/250ml NS or D_3W 20-30 min qh (max 3 doses)	• Atropine 1-2mg IM or 1 auto-inj. q5-10 min qs • 2-PAMCl consider 600mg IM or 1 auto-injector qh (max 3 doses) or • 15mg/kg/250ml NS 20-30 min qh (max 3 doses)	• Atropine 1mg IM q5-10 min qs • 2-PAMCl consider 15mg/kg/250ml NS 20-30 min qh (max 3 doses) or 150-300mg IM	• Atropine 0.5mg IM q5-10 min qs • 2-PAMCl consider 15mg/kg/250ml NS 20-30 min qh (max 3 doses) or 150mg IM
Mild Liquid	• localized sweating • muscle fasciculations at exposure site only • delayed presentation (miosis NOT an early sign) [s & s may be delayed 1-2 hrs]	• Atropine 2mg IM or IV or 1 Auto-inj. q5-10 min qs • 2-PAMCl 600mg IM or 1 auto-injector or 1g/250ml NS or D_3W 20-30 min qh • observe 18 hours	• Atropine 2mg IM or 1 auto-inj. q5-10 min qs • 2-PAMCl 600mg IM or 1 auto-inj. or 1g/250ml NS or D_3W 20-30 min qh (max 3 doses) • observe 18 hours	• Atropine 1-2mg IM or 1 auto-inj. q5-10 min qs • 2-PAMCl 600mg IM or 1 auto-injector or 15mg/250ml NS 20-30 min qh (max 3 doses) • observe 18 hours	• Atropine 1mg IM q5-10 min qs • 2-PAMCl 15mg/kg/250ml NS 20-30 min qh (max 3 doses) or 150-300mg IM • observe 18 hours	• Atropine 0.5mg IM q5-10 min qs • 2-PAMCl 15mg/kg/250ml NS 20-30 min qh (max 3 doses) or 150mg IM • observe 18 hours
Moderate Vapor	Those of Mild Vapor & • respiratory distress-significant • muscle weakness • fasciculations (twitching) • GI effects – nausea – vomiting – diarrhea	• Atropine 4mg IM or IV or 2 auto-inj. q2mg or 1-injector 5-10 min qs • airway support • 2-PAMCl 1200mg IM or 2 Auto-inj or 1g/250ml NS or D_3W 20-30 min qh (max 3 doses)	• Atropine 2-4mg IM or 1-2 auto-injector q2mg or 1-injector 5-10 min qs • airway support • 2-PAMCl 600-1200mg IM or 1 to 2 auto-injector or 1g/250ml NS or D_3W 20-30 min qh (max 3 doses) • observe 18 hours	• Atropine 1-2mg IM q3-5 min qs or 1 auto-injector q5-10 min qs • airway support • 2-PAMCl 600-1200mg IM or 1 to 2 auto-injector or 15mg/kg/250ml NS 20-30 min qh (max 3 doses) • observe 18 hours	• Atropine 1mg IM q3-5 min qs • airway support • 2-PAMCl 15mg/kg/250ml NS 20-30 min qh (max 3 doses) or 150-300mg IM • observe 18 hours	• Atropine 0.5mg IM q3-5 min qs • airway support • 2-PAMCl 15mg/kg/250ml NS 20-30 min qh (max 3 doses) or 150-300mg IM • observe 18 hours
Moderate Liquid	Those of Mild Liquid & • muscle weakness then generalized muscle twitching • nausea • vomiting • diarrhea • headache (Signs/symptoms of Respiratory problems may not be present)	• Atropine 4mg IM or IV or 2 auto-inj. q2mg or 1-injector 5-10 min qs • 2-PAMCl 1200mg IM or 2 auto-inj or 1g/250ml NS or D_3W 20-30 min qh (max 3 doses) • observe 18 hours	• Atropine 2-4mg IM or 1-2 auto-injector q2mg 5-10 min qs • 2-PAMCl 600mg IM or auto-injector or 1g/250ml NS or D_3W 20-30 min qh (max 3 doses) • observe 18 hours	• Atropine 1-2mg IM q3-5 min qs or 1 auto-inj. q5-10 min qs • 2-PAMCl 600mg IM or auto-injector or 15mg/kg/250ml NS 20-30 min qh (max 3 doses) • observe 18 hours	• Atropine 1mg IM q3-5 min qs • 2-PAMCl 15mg/kg/250ml NS 20-30 min qh (max 3 doses) or 150-300mg IM • observe 18 hours	• Atropine 0.5mg IM q3-5 min qs • 2-PAMCl 15mg/kg/250ml NS 20-30 min qh (max 3 doses) or 150-300mg IM • observe 18 hours

EXPOSURE	SIGNS & SYMPTOMS might include the following:	ADULT	ADOLESCENT (≥11 years) (≥35kg [77lb] apx.)	CHILD 7 thru 10 years (apx. 22 to 35kg [50-77lb])	SMALL CHILD 2 thru 6 years (apx. 11 to 22kg [25-50 lb])	INFANT <2 years (<11kg [25lb] apx.)
Severe Vapor or Liquid	Those of Minimal, Mild, & Moderate PLUS • sudden loss of consciousness • seizures • severe respiratory distress or apnea • flaccid muscle paralysis • GI effects	• airway support • Atropine 6mg IM repeat 2mg IV q3-5 mins or 3 auto-inj. q5-10 min qs (may require 15-20mg in 1ˢᵗ 3 hr.) • 2-PAMCl 1800mg IM (600mg in 3 sites) or 3 auto-inj or 1g/250ml NS or D₅W 20-30 min qh (max 3 doses) • Diazepam 10mg IM or 2-5mg IV qs	• airway support • Atropine 4-6mg IM or 2-3 auto-injector q3-5 min qs • 2-PAMCl 600-1200mg IM (600mg in 2 sites) or 1 to 2 auto-injector or 1g/250ml NS or D₅W 20-30 min qh (max 3 doses) • Diazepam 1-3mg q2-5 min (max 10mg)	• airway support • Atropine 2mg IM q3-5 min qs or 2mg auto-inj. q3-10 min qs • 2-PAMCl 600-1200mg IM or 1 to 2 auto-injector or 15mg/kg/250ml NS 20-30 min qh (max 3 doses) • Diazepam 1mg q2-5 min (max 10mg)	• airway support • Atropine 2mg IM q3-5 min qs • 2-PAMCl 15mg/kg/250ml NS 20-30 min qh (max 3 doses) or 150-300mg IM • Diazepam 0.2-0.5mg/kg q2-5 min (max 5mg)	• Atropine 0.5mg IM q3-5 min qs • 2-PAMCl 15mg/kg/250ml NS 20-30 min qh (max 3 doses) or 150mg IM • if >30days old Diazepam 0.2-0.5mg/kg q2-5 min (max 5mg)

Symptoms may NOT occur as indicated. Treat the symptoms the patient presents with. Effects of an initial reaction may lead to a more serious reaction.

"Moderate" symptoms MAY include those under Mild. "Severe" symptoms MAY develop from symptoms under "Mild" and "Moderate", or go directly to "Severe" symptoms.

VAPOR—onset within seconds to minutes
   —peak effects occur within 5-10 minutes of exposure
     (patient will be as bad as they will get within 20 minutes.)
   —presents NO contact hazard to others
   —off-gassing from clothes possible

LIQUID—the greater the exposure amount the shorter the onset time of signs and symptoms
   —clinical signs may not appear for 30 minutes after large percutaneous exposure
   —onset time may be as long as 18 hours after exposure
   —first effect after asymptomatic period may be loss of consciousness
   —large exposure effects within minutes

ATROPIIZATION (drying of nose/mouth secretions and improved respirations)
   —do not use heart rate as an indicator of effectiveness
   —use caution with Atropine IV, if patient is hypoxic

NOTE
Infants and elderly patients who are exposed and present with progressive airway compromise may be given 2mg of Atropine by auto-injector.

ANTIDOTE Distributed by Health Department for CSEPP consists of:
   Atropine in 1mg/ml vial
   2-PAMCI (i.e. Pralidoxime, Protopam®, Protopam Chloride) 1g powder in 20ml vial [3.3ml sterile water in 1g yields 300mg/ml]
   Sterile Water in 10ml vials for 2-PAMCI reconstitution
   Auto-Injector (Mark 1 Kit)   **Atropine** 2mg equivalent/0.7ml with 22-gauge 0.75 - 0.875 inch spring loaded pressure activated needle and plunger
                        Pralidoxime Chloride 600mg/2ml with 22-gauge 0.71 – 0.91 inch spring loaded pressure activated needle and plunger

Arkansas Department of Health - Emergency Management Section (Parette) (Protocol/Antidote) Dev 2/17/00 REVISED 7-17-00

When to Use Auto-Injectors

Use only after the following events have occurred:

* ⭐ Emergency medical personnel have donned personal protective equipment subsequent to recognizing existence of chemical agent hazard in area
* ⭐ Some or all of signs and symptoms of nerve agent poisoning listed are present:
  * unexplained runny nose
  * tightness of chest with difficulty in breathing
  * pinpointed pupils of the eye (miosis)
  * blurred vision
  * drooling, excessive sweating
  * nausea, vomiting, and abdominal cramps
  * involuntary urination and defecation
  * jerking, twitching, and staggering
  * headache, drowsiness, coma, convulsions
  * stoppage of breathing

Treatment

* ⭐ Immediately administer one atropine auto-injector (2 mg), followed by one 2-PAM CL auto-injector (600 mg).
* ⭐ Atropine should be given first; followed immediately by 2-PAM CL.
* ⭐ If nerve agent signs or symptoms are still present after 5–10 minutes (depending on severity), repeat injections.
* ⭐ If signs or symptoms still exist after an additional 10 minutes, repeat injections for a third time.
* ⭐ If signs or symptoms remain after third set of injections, DO NOT give any more antidotes but seek medical help immediately.

If severe signs and symptoms are present:

* ⭐ Administer all three auto-injector kits (atropine and 2-PAM CL) in rapid succession; then medical help should be sought.
* ⭐ Remove secretions, maintain a patient airway and, if necessary, use artificial ventilation.
* ⭐ Morphine, theophylline, aminophylline, or succincylcholine should not be used with 2-PAM CL. Avoid reserpine or phenothiazine-type tranquilizers.

By Paul M. Maniscalco and Hank T. Christen, reprinted from *Understanding Terrorism and Managing the Consequences* (2002), Prentice-Hall, Inc.

★ 2-PAM CL is most effective if administered immediately after exposure. Less effective if given more than 6 hours after termination of exposure.

How To Use Auto-Injectors

The recommended procedure is to inject the contents of the auto-injector into the muscles of an auterolateral thigh (through pocket). Proceed as follows:

1. Remove safety cap (yellow on atropine; gray on 2-PAM CL; both in clip on Mark I). Do not touch the colored end of the injector after removing the safety cap, since the injector can and will function into the fingers or hand if any pressure is applied to this end of the injector.

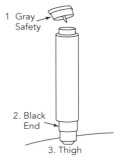

1 Gray Safety

2. Black End

3. Thigh

2. Hold injector as you would a pen. Place colored end (green on atropine, black on 2-PAM CL) on thickest part of thigh and press hard until injector functions. Pressure automatically activates the spring, which plunges the needle into the muscle and simultaneously forces fluid through it into the muscle tissues.

3. Hold firmly in place for ten seconds, then remove. Massage the area of injection.
4. After each auto-injector has been activated, the empty container should be disposed of properly. It cannot be refilled nor can the protruding needle be retracted. It should be disposed of in a "sharps" container in accordance with rules for handling medical wastes and possible blood-borne pathogens.

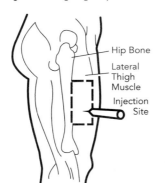

Hip Bone

Lateral Thigh Muscle

Injection Site

Dosage should be noted on a triage tag or written on the chest or forehead of the patient.

IMPORTANT: Physicians and/or other medical personnel assisting evacuated victims of nerve agent exposure should avoid exposing themselves to cross-contamination by ensuring they do not come in contact with the patient's clothing.

CSEPP Recommended Guidelines for Antidote Treatment for Nerve Gas Agent Exposure

★ Laws regulating the use of controlled drugs differ from state to state. In some states atropine or 2-PAM Chloride can only be administered under the direction of a physician. You should be familiar with the laws and local protocols governing drug administration in emergency situations in your state.

★ A MARK I kit contains two auto-injectors: unit 1 contains 2 mg of atropine, and unit 2 contains 600 mg of 2-PAM Chloride.

★ You should identify at least 2 signs and symptoms of nerve agent poisoning before beginning treatment. Doses may be repeated as clinically indicated. Atropine treatment should be repeated until the patient is atropinized. Incremental 2-PAM Chloride dosages may be repeated until the maximum dose based on body weight is achieved.

★ If an adult patient shows mild signs of miosis and rhinorrhea after vapor exposure, experts generally recommend observation only.

★ A slow IV should be administered over a 20–30 minute period in 250 ml of normal saline or 250 ml 5% D/W solution.

Signs and Symptoms

If an adult patient shows mild signs of miosis and rhinorrhea after vapor exposure, experts generally recommend observation only.

Mild Signs and Symptoms

Miosis (pinpoint pupil)
Blurry vision
Chest tightness
Rhinorrhea (runny nose)
Lacrimation (tearing)

Moderate Signs and Symptoms

Above signs/symptoms plus
Significant respiratory distress

GI effects
Muscle weakness
Fasciculations
Excessive lacrimation
Nausea; vomiting; diarrhea; cramps

Severe Signs and Symptoms

Above signs/symptoms plus
Convulsions
Respiratory failure
Loss of consciousness

Treatment of Adults Exposed to Nerve Agent Vapor

Mild signs and symptoms:
>Atropine:
>>2 mg IV or IM (1 auto-injector)
>>Repeat doses at 5 to 10 minute intervals until patient is atropinized.
>2-PAM CL:
>>1 g by slow IV or 600 mg IM (1 auto-injector)

Moderate signs and symptoms:
>Atropine:
>>4 mg IV or IM (2 auto-injectors)
>>Repeat doses at 5 to 10 minute intervals until patient is atropinized.
>2-PAM CL:
>>1 g by slow IV (repeat hourly as needed for up to a total of 3 g in 3 hours) or 1200 mg IM (2 auto-injectors)

Severe signs and symptoms:
>Atropine:
>>6 mg IV or IM (3 auto-injectors)
>>Once hypoxemia is reversed, an additional 2 mg IV at 3 to 5 minute intervals may be required to support airways.

2-PAM CL:

  1 to 2 g by slow IV (repeat hourly as needed for up to a total of 3 g in 3 hours) or 1800 mg IM (3 auto-injector)

Diazepam:

  10 mg IM or 5 mg IV (repeat doses as required)

Treatment for Direct Contact Exposure to Nerve Adults

A person exposed to liquid nerve agent should be treated according to the signs and symptoms as a person exposed to nerve agent vapor. Due to the slower up-take, however, onset of symptoms may be delayed for 1 to 2 hours and some symptoms may not appear until after 6 hours.

Mild signs and symptoms: Onset of sweating and muscle fasciculation at site of exposure 1 to 2 hours after exposure should be treated with:

  Atropine:

    2 mg IM (1 auto-injector)

  2-PAM CL:

    600 mg IM (1 auto-injector) or 1 g slow IV

Moderate signs and symptoms: Onset of GI symptoms more than 6 hours after exposure should be treated with:

  Atropine:

    2 mg IM (1 auto-injector)

  2-PAM CL:

    600 mg IM (1 auto-injector)

Severe signs and symptoms: Same as for vapor exposure.

  Atropine:

    6 mg IM (3 auto-injector)

  2-PAM CL:

    1 to 2 g by slow IV (repeat hourly as necessary for up to 3g in 3 hrs)

Treatment of Adolescents, Children, and Infants

Treatment varies depending on age and body weight of child or adolescent. The adult-size atropine and 2-PAM CL auto-injectors should never be given to infants.

Atropine: (depends on age)

Repeat doses for all age groups as clinically indicated until patient is atropinized.

Less than 2 years:	0.5 mg IV or IM
2 to 10 years:	1 mg IV or IM
Over 10 years or adolescent:	2 mg IV or IM (1 auto-injector)

2-PAM Chloride: (depends on body weight)

Less than 50 lbs. (22.7 kg):	15 mg per kg of bodyweight by slow IV
Over 50 lbs.:	600 mg IM (1 auto-injector)Repeat doses at hourly intervals as clinically indicated (no more than twice).

Diazepam: (depends on age)

Infants over 30 days to children age 5 years:

0.2 mg to 0.5 mg per kg of body weight slowly every 2 to 5 minutes, up to maximum total dose of 5 mg IV or IM

Children over 5 years:

1 mg every 2 to 5 minutes, up to maximum total dose of 10 mg

Terrorism with Ionizing Radiation General Guidance Pocket Guide

Diagnosis: Be alert to the following

- ☆ Acute radiation syndrome (table 2) follows a predictable pattern after substantial exposure or catastrophic events
- ☆ Individuals may become ill from contaminated sources in the community and be identified based on syndromes as specified in table 2 over much longer time periods
- ☆ Specific syndromes of concern, especially with a 2–3 week prior history of nausea and vomiting, are
  - thermal burn-like skin effects without documented thermal exposure
  - immunological dysfunction with secondary infections
  - a tendency to bleed (epistaxis, gingival bleeding, petechiae)
  - marrow suppression (neutropenia, lymphopenia, and thrombocytopenia)
  - epilation (hair loss)

Understanding exposure

- ☆ Exposure may be known and recognized or clandestine through
  - large radiation exposures, such as a nuclear bomb or damage to a nuclear power station
  - small radiation source emitting continuous gamma radiation producing group or individual chronic intermittent exposures (such as radiological sources from medical treatment devices or environmental water or food pollution
- ☆ Exposure to RADIATION may result from any one or combination of the following
  - external sources (such as radiation from an uncontrolled nuclear reaction or radioisotope outside the body)
  - skin contamination with radioactive material ("external contamination")
  - internal radiation from absorbed, inhaled, or ingested radioactive material ("internal contamination")

Confirmation of cases

★ Contact radiation safety officer (RSO) or help
★ For help in projecting clinical effects, contact
  • nuclear medicine physician
  • Medical Radiological Advisory Team (MRAT) at Armed Forces Radiobiology Research Institute (ARI) 301-295-0530
★ Obtain complete blood count
  • absolute lymphocyte count <1000 m³ suggests moderate exposure
  • absolute lymphocyte count <500 mm suggests severe exposure
  • Acute, short-term rise in neutrophil unt
★ Swab mucosa (all body orifices – each naril, both ears, mouth, rectum)
★ Collect 24 hour stool if GI contaminatii considered
★ Collect 24 hour urine if contamination nsidered

Treatment Considerations

★ If trauma is present, treat
★ If external radioactive contaminants are resent, decontaminate
★ If radioiodine (reactor accident) is presei, consider giving prophylactic potassium iodide (Lugol's Solution within 24 hours only (ineffective later)
★ Review http://www.afrri.usuhs.mil or http://www.orau.gov/reacts/guidance.htm

Decontamination Considerations

★ Exposure without contamination requires no decontamination (RSO measurement)
★ Exposure with contamination requires Universal Precautions, removal of patient clothing, and decontamination with water
★ For internal contamination, contact the RSO and/or Nuclear Medicine Physician
★ Treating contaminated patients before decontamination may contaminate the facility: plan for decontamination before arrival

✫ Patient with life-threning condition: treat, then decontaminate
Patient with non-lithreatening condition: decontaminate, then treat

Institutional reporting

✫ If reasonable suspic of a radiation event, contact hospital leadership (Chief of Staff, Hosal Director, etc)
✫ Immediately discus ospital emergency planning implications

Public Health Reporti

✫ Contact local publiealth office (city, county or State)
✫ If needed, contact t FBI (for location of nearest office, see http://www.fbi.govontact/fo/info.htm)

Table 1: IntermittentChronic Exposure and Effect

Headache Fatigue Weakness	1°,2°, 3° burns Eplation Ulceration
Anorexia Nausea Vomiting Diarrhea	Lymphopenia Neutropenia Thrombocytopenia Purpura Opportunistic infections

Table 2: Acute Radiation Syndrome

Phase of Syndrome	Feature	Whole body radiation from external radiation or internal absorption					
		Subclinical range		Sublethal range		Lethal range	
		0-100 rad (cGy)	100-200 rad (cGy)	200-600 rad (cGy)	600-800 rad (cGy)	600-3000 rad (cGy)	>3000 rad (cGy)
Initial or prodromal	Nausea, vomiting	none	5-50%	50-100%	75-100%	90-100%	100%
	Time of onset		3-6 hrs	2-4hrs	1-2 hrs	<1 hr	1 hr <
	Duration		<24 hrs	<24 hrs	<48 hrs	<48 hrs	<48 hrs
	Lymphocyte count			< 1000 at 24 h	<500 at 24h		
	CNS function	No impairment	No impairment	Routine task performance Cognitive impairment for 6-20 hrs	Simple and routine task performance Cognitive impairment for >24 hrs	Progressive incapacitation	
Latent	Duration	> 2 wks	7-15 days	0-7 days	0-2 days	None	
"Manifest illness" (obvious illness)	Signs and symptoms	none	Moderate leuko-penia	Severe leukopenia, purpura, hemorrhage Pneumonia Hair loss after 300 rad (cGy)		Diarrhea Fever Electrolyte disturbance	Convulsions, ataxia, tremor, lethargy
	Time of onset	> 2 wks	> 2 wks	2 days - 2 wks		-3 days	
	Critical period	none	none	4-6 wks		5-14 days	1-48 hrs
	Organ system			Hematopoietic and respiratory (mucosal) systems		GI tract Mucosal systems	CNS
Hospitali-zation	%	0	<5%	90%	100%	100%	100%
	Duration		45-60 days	60-90 days	90+ days	2 weeks	2 days
Fatality	%	0%	0%	0-80%	90-100%	90-100%	100%
Time to death				3 wks - 3 months		1-2 wks	1-2 days

The information in this card is not meant to be complete but to be a quick guide; please consult other references and expert opinion.

October 2001

VA access card:http://www.oqp.med.va.gov/cpg/cpg.htm

DoD access card:http://www.cs.amedd.army.mil/qmo

Produced by the Employee Education System for the Office of
Public Health and Environmental Hazards, Department of Veterans Affairs.

OSHA Protection Requirements

LEVEL OF PROTECTION	EQUIPMENT	PROTECTION PROVIDED	SHOULD BE USED WHEN:	LIMITING CRITERIA

A	RECOMMENDED:
	• Pressure-demand, full-facepiece SCBA or pressure-demand supplied-air respirator with escape SCBA.
	• Fully-encapsulating, chemical-resistant suit.
	• Inner chemical-resistant gloves.
	• Chemical-resistant safety boots/shoes.
	• Two-way radio communications.
	
	OPTIONAL:
	• Cooling unit.
	• Coveralls.
	• Long cotton underwear.
	• Hard hat.
	• Disposable gloves and boot covers.
		The highest available level of respiratory, skin, and eye protection.	• The chemical substance has been identified and requires the highest level of protection for skin, eyes, and the respiratory system based on either:
			  – Measured (or potential for) high concentration of atmospheric vapors, gases, or particulates
			     or
			  – Site operations and work functions involving a high potential for splash, immersion, or exposure to unexpected vapors, gases, or particulates of materials that are harmful to skin or capable of being absorbed through the intact skin.
			• Substances with a high degree of hazard to the skin are known or suspected to be present, and skin contact is possible.
			• Operations must be conducted in confined, poorly ventilated areas until the absence of conditions requiring Level A protection is determined.
				• Fully-encapsulating suit material must be compatible with the substances involved.

LEVEL OF PROTECTION	EQUIPMENT	PROTECTION PROVIDED	SHOULD BE USED WHEN:	LIMITING CRITERIA

B	RECOMMENDED:
	■ Pressure-demand, full-facepiece SCBA or pressure-demand supplied-air respirator with escape SCBA.
	■ Chemical-resistant clothing (overalls and long-sleeved jacket; hooded, one or two-piece chemical splash suit; disposable chemical-resistant one-piece suit).
	■ Inner and outer chemical-resistant gloves.
	■ Chemical-resistant safety boots/shoes.
	■ Hard hat.
	■ Two-way radio communications.
	
	OPTIONAL:
	■ Coveralls.
	■ Disposable boot covers.
	■ Face shield.
	■ Long cotton underwear.
		The same level of respiratory protection but less skin protection than Level A.
		
		It is the minimum level recommended for initial site entries until the hazards have been further identified.
			● The type and atmospheric concentration of substances have been identified and require a high level of respiratory protection, but less skin protection. This involves atmospheres:
			  – With IDLH concentrations of specific substances that do not represent a severe skin hazard;
			    or
			  – That do not meet the criteria for use of air-purifying respirators.
			● Atmosphere contains less than 19.5 percent oxygen.
			● Presence of incompletely identified vapors or gases is indicated by direct-reading organic vapor detection instrument, but vapors and gases are not suspected of containing high levels of chemicals harmful to skin or capable of being absorbed through the intact skin.
				■ Use only when the vapor or gases present are not suspected of containing high concentrations of chemicals that are harmful to skin or capable of being absorbed through the intact skin.
				■ Use only when it is highly unlikely that the work being done will generate either high concentrations of vapors, gases, or particulates or splashes of material that will affect exposed skin.

LEVEL OF PROTECTION	EQUIPMENT	PROTECTION PROVIDED	SHOULD BE USED WHEN:	LIMITING CRITERIA
C	RECOMMENDED: ■ Full-facepiece, air-purifying, canister-equipped respirator. ■ Chemical-resistant clothing (overalls and long-sleeved jacket; hooded, one- or two-piece chemical splash suit; disposable chemical-resistant one-piece suite). ■ Inner and outer chemical-resistant gloves. ■ Chemical-resistant safety boots/shoes. ■ Hard hat. ■ Two-way radio communications. OPTIONAL: ■ Coveralls. ■ Disposable boot covers. ■ Face shield. ■ Escape mask. ■ Long cotton underwear.	The same level of skin protection as Level B, but a lower level of respiratory protection.	● The atmospheric contaminants, liquid splashes, or other direct contact will not adversely affect any exposed skin. ● The types of air contaminants have been identified, concentrations measured, and a canister is available that can remove the contaminant. ● All criteria for the use of air-purifying respirators are met.	■ Atmospheric concentration of chemicals must not exceed IDLH levels. ■ The atmosphere must contain at least 19.5 percent oxygen.
D	RECOMMENDED: ■ Coveralls. ■ Safety boots/shoes. ■ Safety glasses or chemical splash goggles. ■ Hard hat. OPTIONAL: ■ Gloves. ■ Escape mask. ■ Face shield.	No respiratory protection. Minimal skin protection.	● The atmosphere contains no known hazard. ● Work functions preclude splashes, immersion, or the potential for unexpected inhalation of or contact with hazardous levels of any chemicals.	■ This level should not be worn in the Exclusion Zone. ■ The atmosphere must contain at least 19.5 percent oxygen.

Hazard Zones as Defined in the 2000 DOT Emergency Response Guidebook Are:

Hot Zone: Area immediately surrounding a dangerous goods incident that extends far enough to prevent adverse effects from released dangerous goods to personnel outside the zone. This zone is also referred to as exclusion zone, red zone, or restricted zone in other documents.

Warm Zone: Area between Hot and Cold zones where personnel and equipment decontamination and Hot Zone support takes place. It includes control points for the access corridor and thus assists in reducing the spread of contamination. Also referred to as the contamination reduction corridor (CRC), contamination reduction zone (CRZ), yellow zone, or limited access zone in other documents.

Cold Zone: Area where the command post and support functions that are necessary to control the incident are located. This is also referred to as the clean zone, green zone, or support zone in other documents.

Reference—U.S. Department of Transportation, 2000 Emergency Response Guidebook.

Interim Recommendations for the Selection and Use of Protective Clothing and Respirators Against Biological Agents

The approach to any potentially hazardous atmosphere, including biological hazards, must be made with a plan that includes an assessment of hazard and exposure potential, respiratory protection needs, entry conditions, exit routes, and decontamination strategies. Any plan involving a biological hazard should be based on relevant infectious disease or biological safety recommendations by the Centers for Disease Control and Prevention (CDC) and other expert bodies including emergency first responders, law enforcement, and public health officials. The need for decontamination and for treatment of all first responders with antibiotics or other medications should be decided in consultation with local public health authorities.

This INTERIM STATEMENT is based on current understanding of the potential threats and existing recommendations issued for biological aerosols. CDC makes this judgment because:

1. Biological weapons may expose people to bacteria, viruses, or toxins as fine airborne particles. Biological agents are infectious through one or more of the following mechanisms of exposure, depending upon the particular type of agent: inhalation, with infection through respiratory mucosa or lung tissues; ingestion; contact with the mucous membranes of the eyes, or nasal tissues; or penetration of the skin through open cuts (even very small cuts and abrasions of which employees might be unaware). Organic airborne particles share the same physical characteristics in air or on surfaces as inorganic particles from hazardous dusts. This has been demonstrated in military research on biological weapons and in civilian research to control the spread of infection in hospitals.
2. Because biological weapons are particles, they will not penetrate the materials of properly assembled and fitted respirators or protective clothing.
3. Existing recommendations for protecting workers from biological hazards require the use of half-mask or full facepiece air-purifying respirators with particulate filter efficiencies ranging from N95 (for hazards such as pulmonary tuberculosis) to P100 (for hazards such as hantavirus) as a minimum level of protection.
4. Some devices used for intentional biological terrorism may have the capacity to disseminate large quantities of biological materials in aerosols.
5. Emergency first responders typically use self-contained breathing apparatus (SCBA) respirators with a full facepiece operated in the most

protective, positive pressure (pressure demand) mode during emergency responses. This type of SCBA provides the highest level of protection against airborne hazards when properly fitted to the user's face and properly used. National Institute for Occupational Safety and Health (NIOSH) respirator policies state that, under those conditions, SCBA reduces the user's exposure to the hazard by a factor of at least 10,000. This reduction is true whether the hazard is from airborne particles, a chemical vapor, or a gas. SCBA respirators are used when hazards and airborne concentrations are either unknown or expected to be high. Respirators providing lower levels of protection are generally allowed once conditions are understood and exposures are determined to be at lower levels.

Interim Recommendations for the selection and use of protective clothing and respirators against biological agents.

When using respiratory protection, the type of respirator is selected on the basis of the hazard and its airborne concentration. For a biological agent, the air concentration of infectious particles will depend upon the method used to release the agent. Current data suggest that the self-contained breathing apparatus (SCBA) which first responders currently use for entry into potentially hazardous atmospheres will provide responders with respiratory protection against biological exposures associated with a suspected act of biological terrorism.

Protective clothing, including gloves and booties, also may be required for the response to a suspected act of biological terrorism. Protective clothing may be needed to prevent skin exposures and/or contamination of other clothing. The type of protective clothing needed will depend upon the type of agent, concentration, and route of exposure.

The interim recommendations for personal protective equipment, including respiratory protection and protective clothing, are based upon the anticipated level of exposure risk associated with different response situations, as follows:

1. Responders should use a NIOSH-approved, pressure-demand SCBA in conjunction with a Level A protective suit in responding to a suspected biological incident where any of the following information is unknown or the event is uncontrolled:
   - the type(s) of airborne agent(s);
   - the dissemination method;
   - if dissemination via an aerosol-generating device is still occurring or it has stopped but there is no information on the duration of dissemination, or what the exposure concentration might be.

2. Responders may use a Level B protective suit with an exposed or enclosed NIOSH-approved pressure-demand SCBA if the situation can be defined in which:
   - the suspected biological aerosol is no longer being generated;
   - other conditions may present a splash hazard.
3. Responders may use a full facepiece respirator with a P100 filter or powered air-purifying respirator (PAPR) with high efficiency particulate air (HEPA) filters when it can be determined that:
   - an aerosol-generating device was not used to create high airborne concentration,
   - dissemination was by a letter or package that can be easily bagged.

These type of respirators reduce the user's exposure by a factor of 50 if the user has been properly fit tested.

Care should be taken when bagging letters and packages to minimize creating a puff of air that could spread pathogens. It is best to avoid large bags and to work very slowly and carefully when placing objects in bags. Disposable hooded coveralls, gloves, and foot coverings also should be used. NIOSH recommends against wearing standard firefighter turnout gear into potentially contaminated areas when responding to reports involving biological agents.

Decontamination of protective equipment and clothing is an important precaution to make sure that any particles that might have settled on the outside of protective equipment are removed before taking off gear. Decontamination sequences currently used for hazardous material emergencies should be used as appropriate for the level of protection employed. Equipment can be decontaminated using soap and water, and 0.5% hypochlorite solution (one part household bleach to 10 parts water) can be used as appropriate or if gear had any visible contamination. Note that bleach may damage some types of firefighter turnout gear (one reason why it should not be used for biological agent response actions). After taking off gear, response workers should shower using copious quantities of soap and water.

Defense Protective Service

NBC Indicator Matrix

A handout developed by the Defense Protective Service to provide first responders with a tool to assess general indicators that may be present at a Nuclear, Biological, or Chemical incident until such time as a more technical assessment can be made and a process for reporting that assessment to appropriate authorities.

Defense Protective Service
1155 Defense Pentagon
Washington, D.C. 20301-1155
Phone: (703) 695-4088

Instructions for Using NBC Indicator Matrix

The NBC Indicator Matrix process is an assessment of general indicators that may be present at a Nuclear, Biological, or Chemical Incident. Developed for use as part of the Defense Protective Service (DPS) NBC Response Plan, the use of this matrix should not be considered as a authoritative determination of the type of NBC Incident that is occurring, but is rather a general guide for First Responding personnel (police, fire, or medical) until a more technical assessment can be made.

The matrix itself is a combination of symptoms, observations, and other indicators (listed in the order that such indicators are most likely to be noticed) that may be present for each of the agents/materials listed at the top. Primarily designed for use in Communications Centers (911, Dispatch Centers, etc.) or Emergency Operations Centers (fixed or mobile) to record indications in which the indicator would be noticed by first responding personnel to the scene of a potential NBC emergency. However, should these operations centers also be affected by the emergency it is possible for field units to use the matrix as well. The intended result is to give some indication of what type of NBC materials may be involved in the emergency to the initial responding units until such time as a expert determination can be made.

How To Use

(The following steps assume responding units are reporting information to their Dispatchers)

1. Units arrive at scene where even at a distance it is apparent that multiple persons are affected.
2. Units should **"STOP, LOOK, and LISTEN"** and relay observations to their dispatchers (See note on Radio Transmit Code).
3. Dispatcher personnel will record each of the relayed observations on the matrix by placing a check mark in the "Indicator Present" column for each indicator so observed.
4. For every row in which the Indicator Present column is checked the dispatcher will place another check mark in all "underlined">unshaded" boxes (including those with words inside the box) on that row. (Note: Boxes with words are designed to help classify the indicator, for example, vomiting is listed for all NBC materials, but "bloody" vomiting is a sign of blister agent use.)
5. At the bottom of each page the total number of check marks for each column should be added and recorded as page totals and these totals transferred to Page 3 of the matrix. Total up all the page totals listed on

Page 3, and the column with the highest number of indicators should be considered that agent/material most likely present.

Radio transmit code note: For those agencies requiring a means to transmit information over a radio net or by unsecured phone line using code a column marked "Radio Transmit Code" lists a numeric code for each indicator (i.e., 1-1 for Prostration) listed on the matrix. In addition each of the types of NBC materials has an alphabetic letter designation. The use of these matrix codes would require that both the sending unit and the receiving station have the NBC Indicator Matrix available. Examples on possible uses are as follows:

1. "NBC Matrix 1-1 and 2-2" would indicate the prostration and painless blisters indicators were observed.
2. "NBC Matrix 1-9 and 5-7 Bravo" would indicate vomiting and 'bloody' diarrhea indicators were observed.
3. "NBC Matrix Total Indicators Present is 12 with A (Alpha) = 6, B (Bravo) = 4, and G (George) = 3" would indicate that a total of 12 indicators were listed on page 3 with 6 indicators for nerve agents, 4 indicators for blister agent, and 3 indicators for biological agents. This example could be used to transmit indicator totals to another agency using the matrix (such as the USPHS). The rules for using transmit codes or to transmit in the clear is left up to the agency using the matrix.

Special Thanks to the Marietta Fire and Emergency Services and the Georgia Mutual Aid Group (GMAG) for the suggested format change that resulted in a 3 page matrix instead of the original 8 page matrix from earlier editions of 10-90 Gold.

Defense Protective Service
NBC Indicator Matrix

(Place a check mark for each indicator noted at the incident in each unshaded box across the row for that indicator. At bottom of each page total up the number of check marks made for each column and at last page total up all page totals. Highest score is indicator for which NBC material is involved. **For Official Use Only by Police, Fire, and Medical Service Agencies.**)

Indicator Noticed by First Responder *(These indicators are listed in the order in which the indicator would be noticed by first responding personnel to the scene of an NBC Emergency)* **STOP, LOOK and LISTEN** *(Resist rushing in, approach incident from upwind, stay clear of all spills, vapors, fumes and smoke. Be extremely mindful of enclosed or confined spaces.)*	Indicator Present	Radio Transmit Code	Nerve Agent	Blister Agents	Blood Agents	Choking Agents	Irritating Agents	Incapacitating Agents	Biological Agents	Radiological Materials
APPEARANCE (at a distance, multiple persons affected)			A	B	C	D	E	F	G	H
Prostration		1-1								
Involuntary twitching and jerking		1-2								
Convulsions		1-3								
Coma		1-4								
Confusion		1-5								
Bleeding from orifices (nose, ears, mouth, rectum)		1-6								
Coughing		1-7								
Sneezing, violent and persistent		1-8								
Vomiting		1-9	Bloody							
SKIN										
Reddening of lips and skin		2-1								
Blisters, painless (ask victim)		2-2								
Blisters, painful (ask victim)		2-3								
Gray area of dead skin that does not blister		2-4								
Sunburn like appearance (erythema)		2-5								
Pain, stinging or deep aching (ask victim)		2-6								
Clammy skin		2-7								
Skin, lesions, multiple pinpoint		2-8								
Hair Loss, large quantities		2-9								
EYES										
Pinpointing of pupils		3-1								
Enlargement of pupils		3-2								
Lesions		3-3								
Involuntary closing		3-4								
PAGE ONE TOTALS										

Indicator	Code									
Tears or tearing	3-5									
Eyes, immediate burning sensation & gritty feeling	3-6									
Pain in and above eyes, aggravated by bright light	3-7									
Dimness of vision (ask victim)	3-8									
RESPIRATORY										
Coughing-up of frothy sputum	3-9								Bloody	
Severe and uncontrollable coughing	3-10									
Hoarseness, (may progress to loss of voice)	3-11									
Runny Nose - copious	4-1									
Breathing Rate decreased	4-2									
Breathing Rate increased	4-3									
Breathing Depth increased	4-4									
Breathing, difficult (Observed or ask victim)	4-5									
Dry Throat (ask victim)	4-6									
Tightness in chest (ask victim)	4-7									
EXAMINATION (with protection if significant indicators above are found)										
CARDIOVASCULAR										
Pulse slow	4-8									
Blood pressure low	4-9									
Blood pressure high	5-1									
Heart action rapid and feeble	5-2									
Heart beat, rapid	5-3									
Headache (ask victim)	5-4									
Headaches, Frontal (ask victim)	5-5									
Dizziness (ask victim)	5-6									
DIGESTIVE SYSTEM (GI, GU, Glands)										
Diarrhea	5-7	Bloody								
Involuntary defecation and urination	5-8									
Nausea	5-9									
Localized Sweating	5-10									
Excessive Sweating	5-11									
TEMPERATURE										
Fever	6-1									
Temperature, subnormal	6-2									
PAGE TWO TOTALS										

HISTORY or ENVIRONMENTAL	Indicator Present	Radio Transmit Code	Nerve Agent (A)	Blister Agents (B)	Blood Agents (C)	Choking Agents (D)	Irritating Agents (E)	Incapacitating Agents (F)	Biological Agents (G)	Radiological Materials (H)
Odor - Apple Blossom		6-3					■			
Odor - Pepper like		6-4					■			
Odor - Garlic		6-5	■				■			
Odor - Horseradish		6-6	■				■			
Odor - Bitter Almonds (faint)		6-7	■	■	■					
Odor - Sour Fruit		6-8					■			
Odor - Peach kernels (faint)		6-9			■					
Odor - New mown hay or fleshly cut grass		6-10				■				
Odor - Fruity to geranium like		7-1		■						
Unscheduled and unusual spray being disseminated.		7-2	■	■	■	■	■	■	■	
Unusual Liquid Droplets, oily, no recent rain.		7-3	■	■			■	■	■	
Abandoned spray devices		7-4	■	■			■	■	■	
Dead Animals, Birds, Fish.		7-5					■		■	
Dead Weeds, Trees, Bushes, Lawns, etc.		7-6				■				
Illness associated with specific geographic area, i.e. victims have different treatment locations, but all work within same area.		7-7							■	
Immediate Fatalities, not associated with trauma		7-8	■		■				■	
Lack of Insect Life.		7-9	■							
Low Lying Clouds not explained by surroundings.		7-10					■		■	
Reports of colleagues, medical community, media, etc., with similar unexplained illness.		8-1							■	
TOTALS			**A**	**B**	**C**	**D**	**E**	**F**	**G**	**H**
TOTAL INDICATORS FROM PAGE 1										
TOTAL INDICATORS FROM PAGE 2										
TOTAL INDICATORS FROM PAGE 3										
1. Put on Respiratory Protection 2. Report all observations to Communications 3. Report wind conditions (speed & direction) 4. Calm Victims: "Help is on the Way!!!" 5. Direct walking wounded to a collection point 6. Touch nothing and no victim until in PPE 7. REMAIN CALM										
TOTAL INDICATORS OF ALL PAGES										

(Note: This process is an assessment of general indicators and should not be considered as authoritative determination of the type of NBC Incident that is occurring. This process is only a general guide for First Responders until a more technical assessment can be made.)

Comments and/or suggested improvements to this matrix are welcomed. Contact Captain Michael Dougherty, DPS, at (703) 695-4088

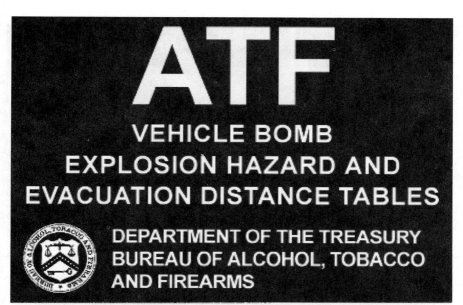

ATF

VEHICLE BOMB EXPLOSION HAZARD AND EVACUATION DISTANCE TABLES

DEPARTMENT OF THE TREASURY BUREAU OF ALCOHOL, TOBACCO AND FIREARMS

IF YOU SUSPECT UNLAWFUL POSSESSION OR USE OF EXPLOSIVES OR BOMBS CALL 1-888-ATF-BOMB OR YOUR LOCAL ATF OFFICE FOR ASSISTANCE

- Minimum evacuation distance is the range at which a life-threatening injury from blast or fragment hazards is unlikely. However, non-life-threatening injury or temporary hearing loss may occur.
- Hazard ranges are based on open, level terrain.
- Minimum evacuation distance may be less when explosion is confined within a structure.
- Falling glass hazard range is dependent on line-of-sight from explosion source to window. Hazard is from falling shards of broken glass.
- Metric equivalent values are mathematically calculated.
- Explosion confined within a structure may cause structural collapse or building debris hazards.
- Additional hazards include vehicle debris.

This information was developed with data from the Dipole Might vehicle bomb research program conducted by ATF, with technical assistance from the U.S. Army Corps of Engineers. Goals for Dipole Might include creating a computerized database and protocol for investigating large-scale vehicle bombs. Dipole Might is sponsored by the Technical Support Working Group (TSWG). TSWG is the research and development arm of the National Security Council interagency working group on counterterrorism.

ATF	VEHICLE DESCRIPTION	MAXIMUM EXPLOSIVES CAPACITY	LETHAL AIR BLAST RANGE	MINIMUM EVACUATION DISTANCE	FALLING GLASS HAZARD
	COMPACT SEDAN	500 Pounds 227 Kilos (In Trunk)	100 Feet 30 Meters	1,500 Feet 457 Meters	1,250 Feet 381 Meters
	FULL SIZE SEDAN	1,000 Pounds 455 Kilos (In Trunk)	125 Feet 38 Meters	1,750 Feet 534 Meters	1,750 Feet 534 Meters
	PASSENGER VAN OR CARGO VAN	4,000 Pounds 1,818 Kilos	200 Feet 61 Meters	2,750 Feet 838 Meters	2,750 Feet 838 Meters
	SMALL BOX VAN (14 FT BOX)	10,000 Pounds 4,545 Kilos	300 Feet 91 Meters	3,750 Feet 1,143 Meters	3,750 Feet 1,143 Meters
	BOX VAN OR WATER/FUEL TRUCK	30,000 Pounds 13,636 Kilos	450 Feet 137 Meters	6,500 Feet 1,982 Meters	6,500 Feet 1,982 Meters
	SEMI- TRAILER	60,000 Pounds 27,273 Kilos	600 Feet 183 Meters	7,000 Feet 2,134 Meters	7,000 Feet 2,134 Meters

Disclaimer

Extensive and reasonable care has been exercised in the preparation of this pocket guide. Biological/Chemical/Radiological/Explosive/Cyber information, references and authorities were utilized to document the applicability of the material herein. This pocket guide is designed and intended to serve as an initial guide to responders and not as a hard and fast set of rules. At the site of any terrorist incident involving any threat agents—military grade, toxic industrial materials or explosives—characteristics and circumstances will vary and are unpredictable. Some incidents may only require the most rudimentary application of the tactics found within while other incidents will require expanded interventions not addressed in this document. The sole purpose intended is to provide the best possible information for a safe and effective initial response to these type events.

The reader is expressly warned to consider and adopt all safety precautions that may be indicated by the activities described herein and to avoid all potential hazards. By following the instructions contained herein, the reader willingly assumes all risks in connect with their actions. Consistent with all hazardous responses always consult at least three references when determining tactical operations.

Every telephone number and internet link was functional at the time of writing.

Material Safety Data Sheet

SECTION I–GENERAL INFORMATION

Date: 14 September 1988
Revised: 28 February 1996

Manufacturer's address:

U.S. ARMY CHEMICAL BIOLOGICAL DEFENSE COMMAND
EDGEWOOD RESEARCH DEVELOPMENT,
AND ENGINEERING CENTER (ERDEC)
ATTN: SCBRD-ODR-S
ABERDEEN PROVING GROUND, MD 20101-5423

Emergency telephone #'s: 0700-1630 EST: 410-671-4411/4414
After: 1630 EST: 410-278-5201, Ask for Staff Duty Officer

CAS registry numbers: 107-44-8, 50642-23-4

Chemical name:

Isopropyl methylphosphonofluoridate

Alternate chemical names:

O-Isopropyl Methylphosphonofluoridate

Phosphonofluoridic acid, methyl-, isopropyl ester

Phosphonofluoridic acid, methyl-, 1-methylethyl ester

Trade name and synonyms:

Isopropyl ester of methylphosphonofluoridic acid
Methylisopropoxfluorophosphine oxide
Isopropyl Methylfluorophosphonate
O-Isopropyl Methylisopropoxfluorophosphine oxide
Methylfluorophosphonic acid, isopropyl ester
Isopropoxymethylphosphonyl fluoride
Isopropyl methylfluorophosphate
Isopropoxymethylphosphoryl fluoride
GB
Sarin
Zarin

Chemical family: Fluorinated organophosphorous compound

Formula/chemical structure:

C4H10F02P

NFPA 704 hazard signal:

Health–4
Flammability–1
Reactivity–1
Special–0

SECTION II–HAZARDOUS INGREDIENTS

INGREDIENTS NAME	FORMULA	PERCENTAGE BY WEIGHT	AIRBORNE EXPOSURE LIMIT (AEL)
GB	C4H10FO2P	100	0.0001 mg/m3

SECTION III–PHYSICAL DATA

Boiling point: 158 C (316 F)

Vapor pressure (mm Hg): 2.9 @ 25 C

Vapor density (air=1): 4.86

Solubility: Miscible with water. Soluble in all organic solvents.

Specific gravity (H$_2$O=1): 1.0887 @ 25 C

Freezing/melting point: –56 C

Liquid density (g/cc):

1.0887 @ 25 C
1.102 @ 20 C

Percentage volatile by volume:

22,000 m/m3 @ 25 C
16,090 m/m3 @ 20 C

Appearance and odor: Colorless liquid. Odorless in pure form.

SECTION IV–FIRE AND EXPLOSION DATA

Flash point (method used): Did not flash to 280 F

Flammable limit: Not applicable

Lower explosive limit: Not available

Upper explosive limit: Not available

Extinguishing media: Water mist, fog, foam, CO2.

Avoid using extinguishing methods that will cause splashing or spreading of the GB.

Special fire fighting procedures: GB will react with steam or water to produce toxic and corrosive vapors. All persons not engaged in extinguishing the fire should be evacuated. Fires involving GB should be contained to prevent contamination to uncontrolled areas. When responding to a fire alarm in buildings or areas containing agents, firefighting personnel should wear full firefighting protective clothing (without TAP clothing) during chemical agent firefighting and fire rescue operations. Respiratory protection is required. Positive pressure, full face piece, NIOSH-approved self-contained breathing apparatus (SCBA) will be worn where there is danger of oxygen deficiency and when directed by the fire chief or chemical accident/incident (CAI) operations officer. In cases where firefighters are responding to a chemical accident/incident for rescue/reconnaissance purposes, they will wear appropriate levels of protective clothing **(See Section VIII)**.

Do not breathe fumes. Skin contact with nerve agents must be avoided at all times. Although the fire may destroy most of the agent, care must still be taken to assure the agent or contaminated liquids do not further contaminate other areas or sewers. Contact with the agent liquid or vapor can be fatal.

Unusual fire and explosion hazards: Hydrogen may be present.

SECTION V–HEALTH HAZARD DATA

Airborne exposure limits (AEL): The permissible airborne exposure concentration for GB for an 8-hour workday or a 40-hour work week is an 8-hour time weighted average (TWA) of 0.0001 mg/m3. This value is based on the TWA of GB which can be found in "AR 40-8, Occupational Health Guidelines for the Evaluation and Control of Occupational Exposure to Nerve Agents GA, GB, GD, and VX." To date, the Occupational Safety and Health Administration (OSHA) has not promulgated a permissible exposure concentration for GB.

GB is not listed by the International Agency for Research on Cancer (IARC), American Conference of Governmental Industrial Hygienists (ACGIH), Occupational Safety and Health Administration (OSHA), or National Toxicology Program (NTP) as a carcinogen.

Effects of overexposure: GB is a lethal cholinesterase inhibitor. Doses that are potentially life threatening may be only slightly larger than those producing least effects.

GB

Route Dosage	Form	Effect	Type
ocular	vapor	ECt50	<2 mg-min/m3
inhalation	vapor	ECt50	<2 mg-min/m3
inhalation (15 1/min)	vapor	ICt50	35 mg-min/m3
inhalation	vapor	LCt50	70 mg-min/m3
percutaneous	liquid	LD50	1700 mg/70 kg man

Effective dosages for vapor are estimated for exposure durations of 2–10 minutes.

Symptoms of overexposure may occur within minutes or hours, depending upon dose. They include: miosis (constriction of pupils) and visual effects, headaches and pressure sensation, runny nose and nasal congestion, salivation, tightness in the chest, nausea, vomiting, giddiness, anxiety, difficulty in thinking and sleeping, nightmares, muscle twitches, tremors, weakness, abdominal cramps, diarrhea, involuntary urination and defecation. With severe exposure symptoms progress to convulsions and respiratory failure.

EMERGENCY AND FIRST AID PROCEDURES:

Inhalation: Hold breath until respiratory protective mask is donned. If severe signs of agent exposure appear (chest tightens, pupil constriction, uncoordination, etc.), immediately administer, in rapid succession, all three Nerve Agent Antidote Kit(s), Mark I injectors (or atropine if directed by physician).

Injections using the Mark I kit injectors may be repeated at 5 to 20 minute intervals if signs and symptoms are progressing until three series of injections have been administered. No more injections will be given unless directed by medical personnel. In addition, a record will be maintained of all injections given. If breathing has stopped, give artificial respiration. Mouth-to-mouth resuscitation should be used when approved mask-bag or oxygen delivery systems are not available. Do not use mouth-to-mouth resuscitation when facial contamination exists. If breathing is difficult, administer oxygen. Seek medical attention IMMEDIATELY.

Eye contact: Immediately flush eyes with water for at least 15 minutes, then don respiratory protective mask. Although miosis (pinpointing of the pupils) may be an early sign of agent exposure, an injection will not be administered when miosis is the only sign present. Instead, the individual will be taken IMMEDIATELY to a medical treatment facility for observation.

Skin contact: Don respiratory protective mask and remove contaminated clothing. Immediately wash contaminated skin with copious amounts of soap and water, 10% sodium carbonate solution, or 5% liquid household bleach. Rinse well with water to remove decontaminant. Administer Nerve Agent Antidote Kit(s), MARK I injectors only if local sweating and muscular twitching symptoms are observed. Seek medical attention IMMEDIATELY.

Ingestion: Do not induce vomiting. First symptoms are likely to be gastrointestinal. IMMEDIATELY administer Nerve Agent Antidote Kit(s), MARK I injector(s). Seek medical attention IMMEDIATELY.

SECTION VI–REACTIVITY DATA

Stability: Stable when pure.

Incompatibility: Attacks tin, magnesium, cadmium plated steel, and some aluminum. Slightly attacks copper, brass, and lead; practically no attack on 1020 steels, Inconel & K-monel.

Hazardous decomposition: Hydrolyzes to form HF under acid conditions and isopropyl alcohol & polymers under basic conditions.

Hazardous polymerization: Does not occur.

SECTION VII–SPILL, LEAK, AND DISPOSAL PROCEDURES

Steps to be taken in case material is released or spilled: If leaks or spills occur, only personnel in full protective clothing will remain in area (See Section VIII). In case of personnel contamination see Section V for emergency and first aid instructions.

Recommended field procedures: Spills must be contained by covering with vermiculite, diatomaceous earth, clay, fine sand, sponges, and paper or cloth towels. Decontaminate with copious amounts of aqueous sodium hydroxide solution (a minimum 10 wt. %). Scoop up all material and clothing and place in a DOT approved container. Cover the contents with decontaminating solution as above. After sealing, the exterior of the container will be decontaminated and then labeled according to EPA and DOT regulations. All leaking containers will be over packed with vermiculite placed between the interior and exterior containers. Decontaminate and label according to EPA and DOT regulations. Dispose of the material according to waste disposal methods provided below. Dispose of decontaminate according to Federal, state and local regulations. Conduct general area monitoring with an approved monitor to confirm that the atmospheric concentrations do not exceed the airborne exposure limits (See Sections II and VIII).

If 10 wt.% aqueous sodium hydroxide solution is not available then the following decontaminants may be used instead and are listed in the order of preference: Decontaminating Agent, DS (DS2), Sodium Carbonate, and Supertropical Bleach Slurry (STB).

Recommended laboratory procedures: A minimum of 56 grams of decon solution is required for each gram of GB. Decontaminant and agent solution is allowed to agitate for a minimum of one hour. Agitation is not necessary following the first hour. At the end of the hour, the resulting solution should be adjusted to a pH greater than 11.5. If the pH is below 11.5, NaOH should be added until a pH above 11.5 can be maintained for 60 minutes. An alternate solution for the decontamination of GB is 10 wt.% sodium carbonate in place of the 10% sodium hydroxide solution above. Continue with 56 grams of decon for each gram of agent. Agitate for one hour but allow three hours for the reaction. The final pH should be adjusted to above zero. It is also permitted to substitute 5.25% sodium hypochlorite or 25 wt. % Monoethylamine (MEA) for the 10% sodium hydroxide solution above. MEA must be completely dissolved in water before addition of the agent. Continue with 56 grams of decon for each gram of GB and provide agitation for one hour. Continue with same ratios and time stipulations. Scoop up all material and clothing and place in a DOT approved container. Cover the contents with decontaminating solution as above. After sealing, the exterior of the container will be decontaminated and then labeled according to EPA and DOT regulations. All leaking containers will be over packed with vermiculite placed between the interior and exterior containers. Decontaminate and label according to EPA and DOT regulations. Dispose of according to waste disposal methods provided below. Dispose of decontaminate according to Federal, state and local regulations. Conduct general area monitoring with an approved monitor to confirm that the atmospheric concentrations do not exceed the airborne exposure limits (See Sections II and VIII).

Waste disposal method: Open pit burning or burying of GB or items containing or contaminated with GB in any quantity is prohibited. The detoxified GB (using procedures above) can be thermally destroyed by incineration in EPA approved incinerators according to appropriate provisions of Federal, state and local Resource Conservation and Recovery Act (RCRA) Regulations.

Note: Some states define decontaminated surety material as an RCRA Hazardous waste.

SECTION VIII–SPECIAL PROTECTION INFORMATION

Respiratory protection:

Concentration	Respiratory protective equipment.
< 0.0001 mg/m3	A full face piece, chemical canister, air purifying protective mask will be on hand for escape. (The M9-, M17-, or M40-series masks are acceptable for this purpose. Other masks certified as equivalent may be used)

| > 0.0001 or =0.2 mg/m3 | A NIOSH/MSHA approved pressure demand full face piece SCBA or supplied air respirators with escape air cylinder may be used.
Alternatively, a full face piece, chemical canister air-purifying protective mask is acceptable for this purpose (See DA PAM 385-61 for determination of appropriate level) |
| > 0.2 or unknown mg/m3 | NIOSH/MSHA approved pressure demand full face piece SCBA suitable for use in high agent concentrations with protective ensemble (See DA PAM 385-61 for examples) |

Ventilation:

Local exhaust: Mandatory. Must be filtered or scrubbed to limit exit concentration to < 0.0001 mg/m3. Air emissions will meet local, state and federal regulations.

Special: Chemical laboratory hoods will have an average inward face velocity of 100 linear feet per minute (lfpm) +/- 10% with the velocity at any point not deviating from the average face velocity by more than 20%. Existing laboratory hoods will have an inward face velocity of 150 lfpm +/- 20%. Laboratory hoods will be located such that cross drafts do not exceed 20% of the inward face velocity. A visual performance test using smoke producing devices will be performed in the assessment of the hoods ability to contain agent GB.

Other: Recirculation of exhaust air from agent areas is prohibited. No connection is allowed between agent areas and other areas through the ventilation system. Emergency backup power is necessary. Hoods should be tested at least semiannually or after modification or maintenance operations. Operations should be performed 20 centimeters inside hood face.

Protective gloves:

Butyl Rubber Glove M3 and M4
Norton, Chemical Protective Glove Set

Eye protection: As a minimum chemical goggles will be worn. For splash hazards use goggles and face shield.

Other protective equipment: For general lab work, gloves and lab coat will be worn with mask readily accessible. In addition, daily clean smocks, foot covers, and head covers will be required when handling contaminated lab animals.

Monitoring: Available monitoring equipment for agent GB is the M8/M9 Detector paper, detector ticket, blue band tube, M256/M256A1 kits, bubbler, Depot

Area Air Monitoring System (DAAMS), Automatic Continuous Air Monitoring System (ACAMS), real time monitoring (RTM), Demilitarization Chemical Agent Concentrator (DCAC), M8/M43, M8A1/M43A2, Hydrogen Flame Photometric Emission Detector (HYFED), CAM-M1, Miniature Chemical Agent Monitor (MINICAM) and the Real Time Analytical Platform (RTAP).

Real-time, low-level monitors (with alarm) are required for GB operations. In their absence, an Immediately Dangerous to Life and Health (IDLH) atmosphere must be presumed. Laboratory operations conducted in appropriately maintained and alarmed engineering controls require only periodic low-level monitoring.

SECTION IX–SPECIAL PRECAUTIONS

Precautions to be taken in handling and storing: When handling agents, the buddy system will be incorporated. No smoking, eating and drinking in areas containing agents are permitted. Containers should be periodically inspected for leaks either visually or by a detector kit).

Stringent control over all personnel practices must be exercised Decontamination equipment will be conveniently located. Exits must be designed to permit rapid evacuation. Chemical showers, eyewash stations, and personal cleanliness facilities must be provided. Wash hands before meals and each worker will shower thoroughly with special attention given to hair, face, neck, and hands, using plenty of soap and water before leaving at the end of the work day.

Other precautions: GB must be double contained in liquid and vapor tight containers when in storage or outside a ventilation hood.

For additional information see "AR 385-61, The Army Toxic Chemical Agent Safety Program," "DA PAM 385-61, Toxic Chemical Agent Safety Standards," and "AR 40-8, Occupational Health Guidelines for the Evaluation and Control of Occupational Exposure to Nerve Agents GA, GB, GD, and VX."

SECTION X–TRANSPORTATION DATA

Proper shipping name: Poisonous liquids, n.o.s.

DOT hazard classification: 6.1, Packing Group I, Hazard Zone A

DOT label: Poison

DOT marking: Poisonous liquid, n.o.s. (Isopropyl methylphosphonofluoridate) UN2810, Inhalation Hazard

DOT placard: Poison

Emergency accident precautions and procedures: See Sections IV, VII and VIII.

Precautions to be taken in transportation: Motor vehicles will be placarded regardless of quantity. Drivers will be given full information regarding shipment and conditions in case of an emergency. AR 50-6 deals specifically with the shipment of chemical agents. Shipments of agent will be escorted in accordance with AR 740-32.

While the Edgewood Research Development, and Engineering Center, Department of the Army believes that the data contained herein are factual and the opinions expressed are those of the experts regarding the results of the tests conducted, the data are not to be taken as a warranty or representation for which the Department of the Army or Edgewood Research Development, and Engineering Center assume legal responsibility. They are offered solely for your consideration, investigation, and verification. Any use of this data and information must be determined by the user to be in accordance with applicable Federal, State, and local laws and regulations.

FOR RESPONDING TO BIOLOGICAL/CHEMICAL THREATS

NOVEMBER 1, 1999

Disclaimer

Extensive and reasonable care has been exercised in the preparation of this document. Biological/chemical information, references and authorities were used to document the applicability of the information contained herein. This document is designed to function only as a guide to incident commanders and not to be used as a hard and fast set of rules. At the scene of any terrorist incident involving chemical/biological threat agents circumstances vary and are unpredictable. Incidents may require only the most rudimentary application of the suggestions made in this document, but may also require extremely complex intervention procedures that are beyond the scope of this document.

Preface

This On-Scene Commander's Guide for Responding to Biological/Chemical Threats has been developed in coordination with "stakeholders" from federal agencies (the "interagency"), and state and local emergency responder communities. It was developed to enhance the previously disseminated guidance distributed as NDPO Bulletins distributed in December 1998 and April 1999. It is a tool to assist commanders in the field in assessing options during the first two hours of an incident involving a potential biological or chemical agent. It is intended to augment existing response policies and not supersede local protocols. This Guide is general in nature and not intended to be a technical guide for emergency responders. The Guide has dual applicability in law enforcement and public safety communities. I sincerely hope you will find this Guide to be beneficial.

Thomas M. Kuker
Director

NDPO...BY AND FOR EMERGENCY RESPONDERS.

Biological Threat Agent Incidents

General incident objectives for responding to known or unknown potential biological threats.

Incident Objectives

★ Remove people from harm's way
★ Assess situation
★ Be cognizant of secondary devices
★ Secure the perimeter, set up operation areas, and establish hazard control zones (i.e., hot, warm and cold zone)
★ Control and identify agents involved
★ Rescue, consider decontamination, triage, treat and transport victims
★ Stabilize incident
★ Avoid additional contamination
★ Secure evidence and treat as a crime scene

On-Scene General Assessment

assessing the situation commanders should consider:

★ Evacuating persons from the potential at-risk areas to minimize potential exposure
★ Number of apparent victims
★ Weather conditions, wind direction, atmospheric conditions, and time of day
Plume direction (vapor/cloud movement)
Types of injuries and symptoms presented (potentially none if a recent biological incident)
nformation from witnesses (what they saw and heard)
xact location of incident (type of occupancy)
ature of agent and type of exposure
afe access route and staging area
ating area and deny entry

Additionally commanders should ensure first responders:

(AWARE)

★ **A**pproach scene from upwind/upgrade

★ **W**ear at least respiratory protection immediately

★ **A**lert other first responders of potentially dangerous conditions

★ **R**estrict entry to area

★ **E**valuate victims' signs/symptoms and alert others

Observe possible indicators of a Biological Threat Agent:

★ Unusual Dead or Dying Animals
  - sick or dying animals, marine life, or people (note: *this condition would not occur in the early stages of an incident*)
★ Unusual Casualties
★ Unusual Liquid, Spray, Powder or Vapor
  - spraying any suspicious devices or packages

Hazard Assessment

Types:

★ Bacteria (e.g., anthrax, plague)
★ Virus (e.g., smallpox, viral hemorrhagic fevers)
★ Toxins (e.g., ricin, botulism)

Bacteria and Virus types are living organisms. They:
  - enter the body via inhalation, ingestion, or breaks in skin.
  - grow and reproduce.
  - can be contagious and cause an epidemic.

Toxins are not living organisms. They:
  - enter the body the same as pathogens.
  - are not contagious.

Characteristics:

★ Requires a dispersion device typically for aerosol generation
★ Non-volatile
★ Is not absorbed through intact skin

⋆ More toxic by weight than chemicals agents and industrial chemicals
⋆ Poses a possible inhalation hazard
⋆ Have a delayed effect ranging from several hours, to days, or weeks
⋆ Are invisible to our senses

On-Scene Assessment

SCENARIO #1 An anonymous caller indicating a biological agent (e.g., Anthrax) threat or envelope (letter unopened or opened; no release).

Personal protective equipment, decontamination and/or prophylaxis treatment should not be required unless hazards or risks are indicated.

⋆ Law enforcement response including local police and FBI agent(s).
⋆ Incident commanders should consider whether full fire department response is needed unless device or suspicious material is present or individuals are symptomatic (notify Health Dept. as local Standard Operating Procedures (SOP) dictate).
⋆ Incident commanders should consider whether full HAZMAT response is needed unless device or suspicious material or individuals are presenting symptoms (notify Health Dept. as local SOP dictate).
⋆ Treat as a crime scene.

Response Strategy

SCENARIO #1 An anonymous caller indicating a biological agent (e.g., Anthrax) threat or envelope (letter unopened or opened; no release).

Personal protective equipment, decontamination, and/or prophylaxis treatment should not be required unless hazards or risks are indicated. Routine law enforcement investigation (similar to a bomb threat).

⋆ Persons in the at-risk area should be rapidly evacuated and evaluated by medical/public health professionals as appropriate.
⋆ Treat as a crime scene.
⋆ Information gathering at the scene (threat assessment to determine credibility of a threat).

★ Screen package/envelope by Bomb Squad to ensure no dispersal mechanism/device inside.

★ Double bag the envelope and place in a suitable container like evidence paint can.

★ Control the material as evidence with documentation of "chain of custody" and follow the FBI plan for laboratory analysis through the local FBI office.

★ Search to confirm no substance or additional package/envelope is present.

★ Assess the building ventilation system to rule out forced entry and tampering.

★ An inspection of the building's ventilation system may be warranted based on the assessment.

★ Attention should be focused on appliances or devices foreign to the surroundings.

On-Scene Assessment

> **SCENARIO #2** A package/envelope/device with a potential threat of a biological agent (present or released).

Suspicious material(s) with a threat of a biological agent should initiate a public safety response including notifications according to existing local SOP:

★ Local Police, Bomb Technicians/Squad and FBI agent(s)
★ Fire, EMS, and HAZMAT units
★ Local and state health and environmental departments
★ Treat as a HAZMAT/crime scene

Response Strategy

> **SCENARIO #2** A package/envelope/device with a potential threat of a biological agent (present or released).

Suspicious material(s) with a threat of a biological agent should initiate a public safety response including notifications according to existing local SOP:

★ Persons in the at-risk area should be rapidly evacuated and evaluated by medical/public health professionals as appropriate.

☆ Treat as a HAZMAT/crime scene.

☆ Follow local protocols for evaluating risk regarding potential explosive device(s).

☆ If an explosive device is not ruled out coordinate efforts with local/ regional Bomb Squad and the local FBI office.

☆ If an explosive device is ruled out evaluate for potential chemical, biological, or radioactive source material.

☆ If radioactive source material appears to be present, follow local plans for requesting additional assistance.

☆ Perimeter security denying entry into crime scene.

☆ Follow Evidence Response Team (ERT) protocols for documenting the crime scene.

☆ Decontamination at the site should only be considered for the individual(s) who came in direct physical contact /inhalation with alleged biological powder.

☆ Remove and double-bag clothes and/or provide on-site shower.

☆ Immediate medical evaluation and transport to a medical facility are usually not indicated. This decision can be made in conjunction with the local health officer based on a threat assessment.

☆ Even in a "true" release, prophylaxis can be temporarily delayed until definitive agent identification is completed.

☆ Clothing of exposed persons should be removed at home and either routinely laundered or double-bagged for evidence purposes based on instructions.

☆ Post-Decontamination considerations:

• Law enforcement personnel should interview all potential victims and document their names, addresses, and phone numbers.

• Decisions to provide treatment for Biological Threat Agents should be made by public health officials.

• Consider mental health of potentially exposed persons.

• It is important that sample results be relayed to exposed victims once available to either initiate additional medical procedure(s) if tests are positive or to eliminate fears and anxiety if tests are negative.

• If explosive devices are ruled out and the evaluation for potential chemical, biological, or radioactive source material is negative then response continues as a law enforcement investigation.

A Glossary of Terms

Anthrax: an infectious, usually fatal disease of warm-blooded animals, especially cattle and sheep, caused by the *bacillus anthracis* bacterium. The toxin that exists as spores can live in the soil. The spores are very resistant in the environment and may survive for decades in certain soil conditions. Spores are dormant forms of a bacterium. Bacterium produces the toxin.

Bacteria: Single celled organisms that multiply by cell division and that can cause disease in humans, plants and animals.

Biological Threat Agents: Living organisms or the materials derived from them that cause deterioration of material. Biological threat agents may be used as liquid droplets, slurry, aerosols, or dry powders.

Biological Threat: the intentional use of biological threat agents as weapons designed to kill or injure humans, animals, or plants, or to damage equipment.

Etiological Agents: living microorganism, or toxin, which causes or may cause human disease.

Evidence Response Team: federal, state, local technically trained law enforcement team to collect and process evidence from the crime scene.

Toxins: toxic substance of natural origin produced by an animal, plant, or microbe. They differ from chemical substances in that they are not manmade. Toxins may include botulism, ricin, and mycotoxins

Chemical Threat Agent Incidents

General incident objectives for responding to known or unknown potential chemical threats.

Incident Objectives

★ Remove people from harm's way
★ Assess situation
★ Be cognizant of secondary devices
★ Secure the perimeter, set up operation areas, establish hazard control zones (i.e., hot, warm and cold zone)
★ Control and identify agents involved
★ Rescue, consider decontamination, triage, treat and transport victims
★ Stabilize incident
★ Avoid additional contamination
★ Secure evidence and treat as a crime scene

On-Scene General Assessment

In assessing the situation commanders should consider:

★ Evacuating persons from the potential at-risk areas to minimize potential exposure
★ Weather conditions, wind direction, atmospheric conditions and time of day
★ Plume direction (vapor/cloud movement)
★ Number of apparent victims
★ Types of injuries and symptoms presented (potentially none if a biological incident)
★ Type of exposure and nature of possible agent
★ Information from witnesses (what they saw and heard)
★ Exact location of incident (type of occupancy)
★ Suggested safe access route and staging area
★ Isolate area and deny entry

Additionally commanders should ensure first responders:

(AWARE)

☆ **A**pproach scene from upwind/upgrade

☆ **W**ear at least respiratory protection immediately

☆ **A**lert other first responders of potentially dangerous conditions

☆ **R**estrict entry to area

☆ **E**valuate victims' signs/symptoms and alert others

Observe possible indicators of a Chemical Threat Agent:

☆ Unusual or Dying Animals
  • lack of insects
☆ Unexplained Casualties
  • multiple victims
  • serious illness
  • nausea, trouble breathing,
  • convulsions
  • definite casualty patterns
☆ Unusual Liquid, Spray or Vapor
  • droplets, oily film
  • unexplained odors
  • low clouds/fog unrelated to weather
☆ Suspicious Devices/Packages
  • unusual metal debris
  • abandoned spray devices
  • unexplained munitions

Hazard Assessment

Characteristics:

☆ Requires a dispersion device typically for aerosol generation.
☆ Requires weaponization.
☆ Can be found as a solid, liquid or gas.
☆ The less volatile the agent the more persistent.
☆ Clinical effects vary from immediate to hours.
☆ Effects of chemical threat agents are affected by:
  • temperature
  • humidity

- precipitation
- wind speed
- nature of terrain and buildings

Types:
- ★ Nerve Agents
- ★ Blister Agents
- ★ Blood Agents
- ★ Choking Agents
- ★ Irritating Agents

The five classes of chemical threat agents all may produce incapacitation, serious injury, and/or death. Dose dependent on each victim. Effects range from mild to deadly.

On-Scene Assessment

> **SCENARIO #3** An anonymous caller indicating a chemical agent threat (no release).

Protective equipment or decontamination and prophylaxis treatment should not be required unless hazards or risks are indicated:

- ★ Law enforcement response including local police and FBI agent(s).
- ★ Incident commanders should consider whether full fire department response is needed unless device or suspicious material is present or individuals are symptomatic (notify Health Dept. as local SOP dictate).
- ★ Incident commanders should consider whether full HAZMAT response is needed unless device or suspicious material or individuals are presenting symptoms (notify Health Dept. as local SOP dictate).
- ★ Treat as a crime scene.

Response Strategy

> **SCENARIO #3** An anonymous caller indicating a chemical agent threat (no release).

Protective equipment or decontamination and prophylaxis treatment should not be required unless hazards or risks are indicated.

Conduct routine law enforcement investigation (similar to a bomb threat):

* ★ Persons in the at-risk area should be rapidly evacuated and evaluated by medical/public health professionals as appropriate.
* ★ Treat as a crime scene.
* ★ Information gathering at the scene (threat assessment to determine credibility of a threat).
* ★ Search to confirm no substance or additional package/envelope is present.
* ★ Assess building ventilation system to rule out forced entry and tampering.
* ★ Inspection of the building ventilation system may be warranted based on the search.

Attention should be focused on appliances or devices foreign to the surroundings.

On-Scene Assessment

SCENARIO #4 A package/device with a potential threat of a chemical agent (present or released).

Suspicious material along with a threat of a chemical device should initiate a public safety response including notifications according to existing local SOP:

* ★ Persons in the at-risk area should be rapidly evacuated and evaluated by medical/public health professionals as appropriate.
* ★ Local Police, Bomb Technicians/Squad and FBI agent(s)
* ★ Fire, EMS, and HAZMAT
* ★ Local and state health and environmental departments
* ★ Treat as a HAZMAT/crime scene

Response Strategy

SCENARIO #4 A package/device with a potential threat of a chemical agent (present or released).

Suspicious material along with a threat of a chemical or release of a chemical device should initiate a public safety response including notifications according to existing local plans:

* ★ Persons in the at-risk area should be rapidly evacuated and evaluated by medical/public health professionals as appropriate.

★ Treat as a HAZMAT/crime scene.

★ Follow local protocols for evaluating risk regarding a potential explosive device(s).

★ Coordinate efforts with local / regional Bomb Squad and the local FBI office if an explosive device is not ruled out.

★ Evaluate for potential chemical, biological, or radioactive source material if an explosive device is ruled out.

★ Follow local plans for requesting additional assistance if radioactive source material appears to be present.

★ Establish perimeter security denying entry into the HAZMAT/crime scene.

★ Follow Evidence Response Team (ERT) protocols.

Personal Response Safety Considerations

★ Wear self protection

★ Wear the highest level of Personal Protective Equipment (PPE) until additional agent information indicates otherwise

★ Be alert for secondary devices

Response Strategy

★ Establish decontamination capability and begin HAZMAT operations

★ Evaluate need to evacuate or protect in place

★ Preserve crime scene

★ Alert hospitals regarding imminent mass casualties; consider use of field hospitals

★ Coordinate control of personnel

★ Restrict scene access

★ Conduct evacuation

★ Provide scene security

★ Estimate number of casualties

★ Arrange for transportation

★ Establish decontamination areas

★ Separate victims with symptoms at triage from those without symptoms

★ Set up separate decontamination sites for civilians and emergency response personnel

A Glossary of Terms

Blister Agent: a chemical agent, also called a vesicant, which causes serve blistering and burns to tissues, skin, eyes, and respiratory tract. Exposure is through liquid or vapor contact. Also, referred to as mustard agents; examples include lewisite and mustard.

Blood Agent: a chemical agent that interferes with the ability of blood to transport oxygen and causes asphyxiation. Examples include cyanogen chloride and cyanide.

Choking Agent: a chemical agent that causes physical injury to the lungs. It may cause the lungs to fill with liquid, which results in lack of oxygen, hence choking on liquids. Examples include chlorine and phosgene.

Evidence Response Team: federal, state, local technically trained law enforcement team to collect and process evidence from the crime scene.

Irritating Agent: a chemical agent, also called riot control agents or tear gas, which causes respiratory distress and tearing designed to incapacitate. Examples include pepper spray and tear gas.

Nerve Agent: a substance that interferes with the central nervous system. Exposure is through liquid contact with the eyes or skin and inhalation of the vapor. Three distinct symptoms associated with nerve agents are pinpoint pupils, headaches, and chest tightness. Examples include sarin, tabun and VX. *Note: Many symptoms are associated with exposure. Victim's severity of exposure, i.e., condition, can be clinically graded by initial symptom/signs at evaluation and during repeat exam.*

NOTIFICATION

Local law enforcement   _____

Local fire department   _____

Local FBI field office   _____

TELEPHONE LIST

The following list of telephone numbers is provided as suggested contacts for incident commanders. The toll free number to the NRC* is for use after initial notifications are made, and for supplemental guidance.

Local Health Office   _____

Poison Control   _____

Local Emergency Department   _____

State Health Department   _____

National Response Center*   (800) 424-8802

   or

National Response Center (DC area) (202) 267-2675

Other local number   _____

Other local number   _____

Other local number   _____

* The National Response Center (NRC) provides direction to the first response community through the FBI's Weapons of Mass Destruction Operations Unit during suspected terrorist incidents. The WMDOU can initiate the appropriate federal assets in response to the potential WMD threat.

Useful References and Links

REFERENCES:

☆ NDPO Special Bulletin #1 (SB-1)

☆ Medical Management of Biological Casualties—U.S.A.M.R.I.I.D.

☆ Morbidity & Mortality Weekly Report—Bioterrorism Alleging Use of Anthrax & Interim Guidelines for Management, 1998

LINKS:

CDC . . . . www.cdc.gov/
EPA . . . . www.epa.gov/swercepp/
FEMA . . . . www.fema.gov
HHS . . . . http://ndms.dhhs.gov
NDPO . . . . www.ndpo.usdoj.gov
NICI . . . . www.nici.org
NGB . . . . www.ngb.dtic.mil/
OJP . . . . www.ojp.usdoj.gov/osldps
SBCCOM . . . . . . www.apgea.mil/index.html

FEMA—Guide for All-Hazard Emergency Operations Planning

STATE AND LOCAL GUIDE (101), CHAPTER 6,
ATTACHMENT G—TERRORISM
FEDERAL EMERGENCY MANAGEMENT AGENCY

APRIL 2001 **PAGE 6-G-1**

TAB D Incident Indications and First Responder Concerns

> **NOTE:** Extensive additional information on weapons of mass destruction (WMD) hazards and response, including information addressing first responder concerns, is available from various commercial publishers.

A. BIOLOGICAL

1. Indications. Indicators that a WMD incident involving biological agents has taken place may take days or weeks to manifest themselves, depending on the biological toxin or pathogen involved. The Centers for Disease Control and Prevention (CDC) recently developed the following list of epidemiologic clues that may signal a bio-terrorist event:

a. Large number of ill persons with a similar disease or syndrome.
b. Large numbers of unexplained disease, syndrome, or deaths.
c. Unusual illness in a population.
d. Higher morbidity and mortality than expected with a common disease or syndrome.
e. Failure of a common disease to respond to usual therapy.
f. Single case of disease caused by an uncommon agent.
g. Multiple unusual or unexplained disease entities coexisting in the same patient without other explanation.
h. Disease with an unusual geographic or seasonal distribution.
i. Multiple atypical presentations of disease agents.
j. Similar genetic type among agents isolated from temporally or spatially distinct sources.
k. Unusual, atypical, genetically engineered, or antiquated strain of agent.
l. Endemic disease with unexplained increase in incidence.
m. Simultaneous clusters of similar illness in noncontiguous areas, domestic or foreign.

n. Atypical aerosol, food, or water transmission.
o. Ill people presenting near the same time.
p. Deaths or illness among animals that precedes or accompanies illness or death in humans.
q. No illness in people not exposed to common ventilation systems, but illness among those people in proximity to the systems.

2. First Responder Concerns

a. The most practical method of initiating widespread infection using biological agents is through aerosolization, where fine particles are sprayed over or upwind of a target where the particles may be inhaled. An aerosol may be effective for some time after delivery, since it will be deposited on clothing, equipment, and soil. When the clothing is used later, or dust is stirred up, responding personnel may be subject to "secondary" contamination.
b. Biological agents may be able to use portals of entry into the body other than the respiratory tract. Individuals may be infected by ingestion of contaminated food and water, or even by direct contact with the skin or mucous membranes through abraded or broken skin. Use protective clothing or commercially available Level C clothing. Protect the respiratory tract through the use of a mask with biological high-efficiency particulate air (HEPA) filters.
c. Exposure to biological agents, as noted above, may not be immediately apparent. Casualties may occur minutes, hours, days, or weeks after an exposure has occurred. The time required before signs and symptoms are observed is dependent on the agent used. While symptoms will be evident, often the first confirmation will come from blood tests or by other diagnostic means used by medical personnel.

B. CHEMICAL

1. Indications. The following may indicate a potential chemical WMD has been released. There may be one or more of these indicators present.

a. An unusually large or noticeable number of sick or dead wildlife. These may range from pigeons in parks to rodents near trash containers.
b. Lack of insect life. Shorelines, puddles, and any standing water should be checked for the presence of dead insects.
c. Considerable number of persons experiencing water-like blisters, weals (like bee-stings), and/or rashes.
d. Numbers of individuals exhibiting serious heath problems, ranging from nausea, excessive secretions (saliva, diarrhea, vomiting), disorientation, and difficulty breathing to convulsions and death.

e. Discernable pattern to the casualties. This may be "aligned" with the wind direction or related to where the weapon was released (indoors/outdoors).

f. Presence of unusual liquid droplets, e.g., surfaces exhibit oily droplets or film or water surfaces have an oily film (with no recent rain).

g. Unscheduled spraying or unusual application of spray.

h. Abandoned spray devices, such as chemical sprayers used by landscaping crews.

i. Presence of unexplained or unusual odors (where that particular scent or smell is not normally noted).

j. Presence of low-lying clouds or fog-like condition not compatible with the weather.

k. Presence of unusual metal debris—unexplained bomb/munitions material, particularly if it contains a liquid.

l. Explosions that disperse or dispense liquids, mists, vapors, or gas.

m. Explosions that seem to destroy only a package or bomb device.

n. Civilian panic in potential high-profile target areas (e.g., government buildings, mass transit systems, sports arenas, etc.).

o. Mass casualties without obvious trauma.

2. First Responder Concerns. The first concern must be to recognize a chemical event and protect the first responders. Unless first responders recognize the danger, they will very possibly become casualties in a chemical environment. It may not be possible to determine from the symptoms experienced by affected personnel which chemical agent has been used. Chemical agents may be combined and therefore recognition of agents involved becomes more difficult.

C. NUCLEAR/RADIOLOGICAL

1. Indications. Radiation is an invisible hazard. There are no initial characteristics or properties of radiation itself that are noticeable. Unless the nuclear/radiological material is marked to identify it as such, it may be some time before the hazard has been identified as radiological.

2. First Responder Concerns. While there is no single piece of equipment that is capable of detecting all forms of radiation, there are several different detectors for each type of radiation. Availability of this equipment, in addition to protective clothing and respiratory equipment, is of great concern to first responders.

TAB E Potential Areas of Vulnerabllity

Areas at risk may be determined by several points: population, accessibility, criticality (to everyday life), economic impact, and symbolic value. The identification of such vulnerable areas should be coordinated with the Federal Bureau of Investigation (FBI).

Traffic Determine which roads/tunnels/bridges carry large volumes of traffic. Identify points of congestion that could impede response or place citizens in a vulnerable area. Note time of day and day of week this activity occurs.

Trucking and Transport Activity Note location of hazardous materials (HazMat) cargo loading/unloading facilities. Note vulnerable areas such as weigh stations and rest areas this cargo may transit.

Waterways Map pipelines and process/treatment facilities (in addition to dams already mentioned). Note berths and ports for cruise ships, roll-on/roll-off cargo vessels, and container ships. Note any international (foreign) flagged vessels (and cargo they carry) that conduct business in the area.

> **NOTE:** The Harbor and Port Authorities, normally involved in emergency planning, should be able to facilitate obtaining information on the type of vessels and the containers they carry.

Airports Note information on carriers, flight paths, and airport layout. Annotate location of air traffic control (ATC) tower, runways, passenger terminal, and parking areas.

Trains/Subways Note location of rails and lines, interchanges, terminals, tunnels, and cargo/passenger terminals. Note any HazMat material that may be transported via rail.

Government Facilities Note location of Federal/State/local government offices. Include locations of post office, law enforcement stations, EMS/fire/rescue, town/city hall, and local mayor/governor's residences. Note judicial offices and courts as well.

Recreation Facilities Map sports arenas, theaters, malls, and special interest group facilities.

Other Facilities Map location of financial institutions and the business district. Make any notes on the schedule business/financial district may follow. Determine if shopping centers are congested at certain periods.

Military Installations Note location and type of military installations.

HazMat Facilities, Utilities, and Nuclear Facilities Map location of these facilities.

> **NOTE:** Security and emergency personnel representing all of the above facilities should work closely with local and State personnel for planning and response.

United States Fire Administration

THE CRITICAL INFRASTRUCTURE PROTECTION PROCESS

Job Aid

(Developed by NATEK Incorporated for USFA)

Critical Infrastructure Protection Information Center

16825 South Seton Avenue

Emmitsburg, MD 21727

301-447-1325

usfacipc@fema.gov

www.usfa.fema.gov/cipc

Edition 1: May 2002

I. INTRODUCTION

A. Background

1. Presidential Decision Directive 63z (PDD 63) was issued May 1998 in response to concerns about potential attacks against critical infrastructures.
2. PDD 63 defined critical infrastructures as the physical and cyber systems so vital to the operations of the United States that their incapacity or destruction would seriously weaken national defense, economic security, or public safety.
3. The directive designated the Federal Emergency Management Agency (FEMA) lead agency for the fire and emergency medical services (EMS) community.
4. FEMA directed the U.S. Fire Administration (USFA) to increase critical infrastructure protection (CIP) awareness throughout the fire and EMS community.

B. Fire and Emergency Medical Services Community

1. PDD 63 identified the Emergency Services Sector as one of eight critical infrastructures.
2. The fire and EMS community as well as the law enforcement community comprise the Emergency Services Sector.
3. USFA is the lead critical infrastructure protection (CIP) agency for the fire and EMS community.

C. Job Aid Purpose

1. This Job Aid is a guide to assist leaders of the fire and EMS community with the process of critical infrastructure protection.
2. The document intends only to provide a model process or template for the systematic protection of critical infrastructures.
3. It is not a CIP training manual or a complete roadmap of procedures to be strictly followed.
4. The CIP process described in this document can be easily adapted to assist the infrastructure protection objectives of any community, service, agency, or organization.

II. CIP OVERVIEW

A. Premise

1. Attacks on the physical and cyber systems of fire and emergency services departments will weaken performance or prevent operations.
2. There are three different types of possible attacks:
    a. ***Deliberate*** attacks are caused by people (e.g., terrorists, other criminals, hackers, delinquents, employees, etc.).
    b. ***Natural*** attacks are caused by nature (e.g., hurricanes, tornadoes, earthquakes, floods, wildfires, etc.).
    c. ***Accidental*** attacks are caused by HazMat accidents involving nuclear, biological, or chemical substances.
3. These attacks are serious "*threats*" against critical infrastructures.

B. Objectives

1. To protect the people, physical entities, and cyber systems that are indispensably necessary for survivability, continuity of operations, and mission success.
2. To deter or mitigate attacks on critical infrastructures by people (e.g., terrorists, hackers, etc.), by nature (e.g., hurricanes, tornadoes, etc.), and by HazMat accidents.

C. Philosophy

1. Among all the important procedures or things involved in emergency preparedness, CIP is possibly the most essential component.
2. There will probably never be enough resources (i.e., dollars, personnel, time, and materials) to achieve total emergency preparedness.
3. Senior Fire and EMS leaders must make tough decisions about what department assets really need protection by the application of scarce resources.
4. There should be no tolerance for waste and misguided spending in the business of emergency preparedness and infrastructure protection.
5. From a municipal perspective, the CIP philosophy is to first protect those infrastructures absolutely required for citizen survivability and continuity of crucial community operations.
6. For the community emergency services, the corresponding CIP philosophy is to first protect those infrastructures absolutely required for the survivability of emergency first responders and the success of their missions.
7. It is impossible to prevent all attacks (e.g., terrorism, natural disasters) against critical infrastructures.
8. CIP can reduce the chances of some future attacks, make it more difficult for the attacks to succeed or degrade infrastructures, and mitigate the outcomes when they do occur.

9. Activities to protect assets essential for the accomplishment of missions affecting life and property are proactive, preemptive, and deterrent in nature, which is exactly what critical infrastructure protection is meant to be.

D. Psychology

1. CIP can be a tool to produce an American "mindset" of protection awareness and confidence in our nation's security and prosperity. Given these new thoughts, it may evoke behaviors that are fully supportive and cooperative with necessary protective measures.
2. CIP may also be a means to change the behavior of terrorists. The proper protection of American critical infrastructures has the potential to develop a new "mindset" among terrorists that their actions will be futile and not yield the results they seek.
3. Community leaders and department chiefs should make occasional public announcements that their critical infrastructures are being protected. This must be done without divulging any details that would be useful to adversaries. Such announcements are not intended to be a ruse or disinformation campaign, but an honest declaration for the "psychological" benefit of both friends and foes.

E. CIP Process Preface

1. CIP involves the application of a systematic analytical process fully integrated into all fire and EMS department plans and operations.
2. It is a security related, time efficient, and resource-restrained practice intended to be repeatedly used by department leaders.
3. The CIP process can make a difference only if applied by department leaders, and periodically reapplied when there have been changes in physical entities, cyber systems, or the general environment.
4. It consists of the following five steps:
   a. *Identifying critical infrastructures* essential for the accomplishment of sector missions (e.g., fire suppression, EMS, HazMat, search and rescue, and extrication).
   b. *Determining the threat* against those infrastructures.
   c. *Analyzing the vulnerabilities* of threatened infrastructures.
   d. *Assessing risk* of the degradation or loss of a critical infrastructure.
   e. *Applying countermeasures* where risk is unacceptable.

III. CIP Process Methodology

A. Identifying Critical Infrastructures

1. Identifying critical infrastructures is the first step of the CIP process.
2. The remaining steps of the CIP process cannot be initiated without the accurate identification of a department's critical assets.
3. Critical infrastructures are those physical and cyber assets essential for the accomplishment of missions affecting life and property.
4. They are the people, things, or systems that will seriously degrade or prevent survivability and mission success if not intact and operational.
5. The following are some examples of critical infrastructures:
   a. Fire fighters and EMS personnel.
   b. Fire and EMS stations, apparatus, and communications.
   c. Public Safety Answering Points (or 9-1-1 Centers).
   d. Computer-aided dispatch and computer networks.
   e. Pumping stations and water reservoirs for major urban areas.
   f. Major roads and highways serving large population areas.
   g. Bridges and tunnels serving large population areas.
   h. Regional or local medical facilities.
6. Despite many similarities, the differences in physical and cyber systems among individual departments necessitate that senior leaders identify their own critical infrastructures.
7. Remember that protection measures cannot be implemented if what needs protection is unknown!
8. The Fire Department of New York continued to serve the citizens of New York City following the collapse of the World Trade Center towers. However, their ability to do so was tremendously degraded for a period of time given the unprecedented losses of personnel and equipment—the foremost among critical infrastructures.

B. Determining the Threat

1. Determining the threat against identified critical infrastructures is the second step of the CIP process.
2. A threat is the potential for an attack from people, nature, HazMat accident, or a combination of these.
3. The remaining steps of the CIP process depend upon whether or not a department's critical infrastructures are threatened.
4. A determination of credible threat must be made for each critical infrastructure identified in step one.
5. If there is no threat of an attack against one of a department's critical infrastructures, then the CIP process can stop here for that particular asset.

6. If there is only a low threat against one of a department's critical infrastructures (e.g., an earthquake), then leaders can choose to continue the CIP process or stop it here for that particular infrastructure.
7. When there is a credible threat of an attack against a department's critical infrastructures, then it is necessary to determine the following prior to proceeding to the next step of the CIP process:
   a. Exactly which critical infrastructures are threatened?
   b. By whom or what is each of these infrastructures threatened?
8. Two examples of credible threats against critical infrastructures:
   a. "National intelligence assets warn that suspected terrorists may attempt to steal fire trucks or ambulances."
   b. "Police cite increasing incidents of juvenile delinquents breaking into water pumping stations and tampering with equipment."
9. Leaders should concentrate only on those threats that will dangerously degrade or prevent survivability and mission accomplishment.
10. Resources should be applied to protect only those infrastructures for which a credible threat exists!

C. Analyzing the Vulnerabilities

1. Analyzing the vulnerabilities of credibly threatened infrastructures is the third step of the CIP process.
2. This step requires an examination of the security vulnerabilities (or weaknesses) in each of the threatened infrastructures.
3. A vulnerability is a weakness in a critical infrastructure that renders the infrastructure susceptible to degradation or destruction.
4. There are two types of vulnerabilities to consider in the CIP process:
   a. A weakness in a critical infrastructure that renders the infrastructure susceptible to disruption or loss from a deliberate attack by human adversaries.
   b. A weakness in a critical infrastructure that will further weaken or completely deteriorate as a result of a natural or accidental attack (i.e., natural disaster or HazMat accident).
5. An efficient vulnerability analysis will examine each credibly threatened infrastructure from the "threat point of view."
6. The analysis will seek to understand the ways by which threats from adversaries, nature, or HazMat accidents might disrupt or destroy the examined infrastructure.
7. If a threatened infrastructure has no vulnerabilities, then the CIP process can stop here for that particular infrastructure.
8. The CIP process should proceed to the fourth step only for those threatened infrastructures having vulnerabilities.
9. The following are two examples of vulnerabilities:

    a. Public Safety Answering Points (PSAPs or 9-1-1 Communication Centers) because of their physical locations, power sources, line routing, Internet-based controls of switching, etc.

    b. Computer Aided Dispatch (CAD) because of its network connections with Internet connectivity.

10. The protection of threatened and vulnerable infrastructures cannot be accomplished without knowing what or where the vulnerabilities are!

D. Assessing Risk

1. Assessing risk of the degradation or loss of a critical infrastructure is the fourth step of the CIP process.

2. The following priority guidance applies for this assessment:

    a. Threatened and vulnerable infrastructures are a high priority for the application of countermeasures.

    b. Infrastructures that are either threatened or vulnerable, but not both, are a low priority for protective measures.

3. Focusing on each high priority infrastructure, decision makers must evaluate the cost of countermeasures in terms of available resources (e.g., personnel, time, money, materials).

4. The determined costs of protective measures (doing something) for each high priority infrastructure are now weighed against the impact of the degradation or loss of that infrastructure (doing nothing).

5. Risk is unacceptable if the impact of the degradation or loss of an infrastructure (doing nothing) is considered catastrophic. The CIP process, therefore, must proceed to the final step for the immediate application of countermeasures.

6. If the impact of the degradation or loss of an infrastructure is not considered great, then decision makers can temporarily decide to accept risk until resources become available.

7. For the infrastructures that are risk adverse and require protection, community leaders should decide the order in which they will receive the allocation of resources and application of countermeasures.

8. For example, research reveals that water pumping stations in rural America are notoriously unprotected. If department leaders follow the CIP process and determine the community pumping station to be a high priority infrastructure, then they should not accept risk and seek local government assistance to apply countermeasures as soon as possible.

9. Failure to assess risk can result in the inefficient application of resources and a subsequent reduction in operational effectiveness!

E. Applying Countermeasures

1. Applying countermeasures where risk is unacceptable is the fifth step of the CIP process.

2. Countermeasures are any protective actions that reduce or prevent the degradation or loss of a critical infrastructure to an identified threat.
3. Countermeasures protect infrastructures and preserve the ability of emergency first responders to efficiently perform their services.
4. They are measures of protection applied to high priority infrastructures that necessitate the allocation of resources.
5. Possible countermeasures differ in terms of feasibility, expense, and effectiveness
6. Countermeasures can be simple or complex actions limited only by imagination and creativity.
7. In few instances, there may be no effective means to protect a critical infrastructure. Sometimes, prohibitive costs or other factors make the application of countermeasures impossible.
8. Decisions requiring the application of countermeasures will influence personnel, time, and material resources as well as drive the security budget.
9. The following are two examples of countermeasures:
   a. To protect their personnel infrastructure, all FDNY digital radios will be inexpensively reprogrammed so that one channel will override all others and emit a long tone to warn each fire fighter to immediately evacuate a building.
   b. To protect both their personnel and equipment, a growing number of departments are keeping their apparatus bay doors closed at all times.
10. High priority infrastructures should be considered a loss to plans and operations if not protected by countermeasures!

IV. CIP Process Question Navigator

DIRECTIONS: Answer questions for each infrastructure.

★ Is the person, thing, or system part of the organization's infrastructure?

★ If the answer is **NO**, stop here; but if it is **YES**, then:

★ Is this infrastructure essential for survivability and mission success?

★ If the answer is **NO**, stop here; but if it is **YES**, then:

★ Is there potential for a deliberate, natural, or accidental attack against this critical infrastructure?

★ If the answer is **NO**, stop here; but if it is **YES**, then:

★ Is the threat of an attack against this critical infrastructure a truly credible one?

★ If the answer is **NO**, stop here; but if it is **YES**, then:

☆ Is there a security vulnerability (or weakness) in the threatened critical infrastructure?

☆ If the answer is **NO**, stop here; but if it is **YES**, then:

☆ Does this vulnerability (or weakness) render the critical infrastructure susceptible to disruption or loss?

☆ If the answer is **NO**, stop here; but if it is **YES**, then:

☆ Is it acceptable to assume risk and delay the allocation of resources and the application of countermeasures?

☆ If the answer is **YES**, stop here; but if it is *NO*, then:

☆ Apply countermeasures to protect this critical infrastructure as soon as available resources permit.

V. Infrastructure Protection Decision Matrix

DIRECTIONS: Complete the matrix for each infrastructure.

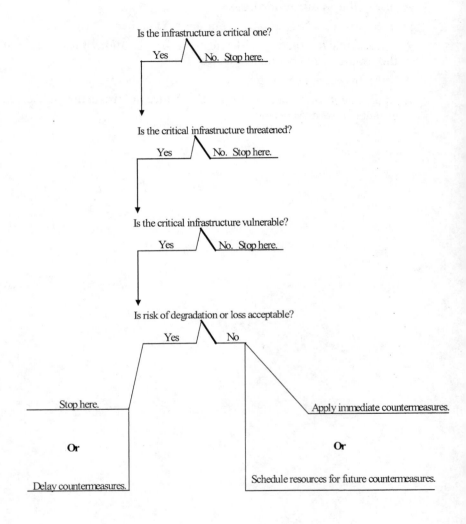

VI. Establishing a CIP Program

A. Justification

1. A quality CIP program supports the protection of the people, physical entities, and cyber systems upon which survivability, continuity of operations, and mission accomplishment depend.
2. The terrorist attacks of 11 September 2001 should provide all senior leaders with sufficient justification to immediately implement a critical infrastructure protection (CIP) program within their organizations.
3. If the threat of terrorism itself does not motivate action, then remember that the CIP process also mitigates or eliminates the devastation of critical assets caused by nature and HazMat accidents.

B. Program Manager

1. Critical infrastructure protection is primarily leader business. The department chief, commander, or director appoints a program manager from among the senior leadership of the organization.
2. The program manager administers the CIP program and maintains its value, relevance, and currency.
3. The program manager prepares, obtains approval for, and publishes the program's purpose, strategic goals, and immediate objectives.
4. The program manager proactively initiates actions that protect the organization's critical infrastructures from deliberate, natural, or accidental attacks.

C. Program Development and Management

1. The department chief, commander, or director institutes the organization's CIP program and delegates authority to a manager.
2. The following program development and management steps are recommended:
   a. Select the program manager from among the senior decision-makers of the organization.
   b. Firmly establish the relationship between the organization's mission and the purpose for critical infrastructure protection.
   c. Win support of the department senior and junior leadership, and orient the CIP program to them.
   d. Focus the program on the practice of the CIP process.
   e. After determining which critical infrastructures must receive immediate protection, aggressively seek the resources required to apply countermeasures as soon as possible.
   f. Revise and reissue the department security policy to include the CIP Program and the critical infrastructures that demand countermeasures.

g. Brief all department personnel regarding the revised policy and ensure awareness of actions they can take to bolster applied protective measures.

h. Practice operations security (protecting sensitive information) concurrently with CIP.

i. Remain vigilant for threat advisories and new CIP trends, methods, and conditions.

j. Maintain the program by reapplying the CIP process when there have been changes in the physical entities, cyber systems, or the general environment; however, attempt to do so at least semi-annually.

3. The USFA CIPIC will provide assistance (via telephone, electronic mail, or facsimile) to any organization establishing a CIP program. Contact the CIPIC by telephone at 301-447-1325, or by electronic mail at: usfacipc@fema.gov. If interested, visit the CIPIC website at: www.usfa.fema.gov/cipc.

ALS	advanced life support
APR	air purifying respirator
ATF	Alcohol, Tobacco, and Firearms
BLS	basic life support
B-NICE	biological, nuclear, incendiary, chemical or explosives.
BSI	body substance isolation
CAS	Chemical Abstract Service
CBR	chemical, biological and radiological
C3I	command, control, communications, and intelligence (C cubed I)
CNS	central nervous system
CPE	chemical protective ensemble
CS, CN	riot control agents
DFO	disaster field office
DMAT	Disaster Medical Assistance Team
DHHS	Department of Health and Human Services
DoD	Department of Defense
DoJ	Department of Justice
DoT	Department of Transportation
EOC	emergency operations center
EOD	explosive ordnance disposal
ERT	emergency response team
ESF	emergency support functions
EMS	emergency medical services
EMT	emergency medical technician
EOP	emergency operations plan
FBI	Federal Bureau of Investigation
FEMA	Federal Emergency Management Agency
FRP	Federal Response Plan
GA,GB,GD	G series nerve agents
HEICS	hospital emergency incident command system
HRT	hostage rescue team
IAP	incident action plan
IDLH	immediate danger to life and health.
ICP	incident command post
ICS	incident command system
IMS	incident management system (interchangeable with ICS)
JOC	joint operations center (FBI)
LACES	lookout, awareness, communications, escape, safety
LEICS	law enforcement command system
LD50	lethal dose, fifty percent
LEL	lower explosive limit
M8	chemical agent detector paper

M256	A kit that detects and identifies vapor concentrations of nerve, blister and blood agents
MACC	multi agency coordination center
MCI	mass casualty incident
MMST	metropolitan medical strike team
MSDS	Material Safety Data Sheets
NDPO	National Domestic Preparedness Office
NMRT	national medical response team
NBC	nuclear, biological, and chemical weapons
NIOSH	National Institutes for Occupational Safety and Health
OSHA	Occupational Safety and Health Administration
PEL	permissible exposure limits
PPE	personal protective equipment
PDD	presidential decision directive
PIO	public information officer
RESTAT	resource status unit
ROC	regional operations center
S-1	military administration officer
S-2	military intelligence officer
S-3	military operations/planning officer
S-4	military logistics officer
SABA	supplied air breathing apparatus
SAC	special agent in charge (FBI)
SCBA	self-contained breathing apparatus
SERT	special emergency response team
SITSTAT	situation status unit
SOP	standard operating procedure
START	simple treatment and rapid triage
SWAT	special weapons and tactics
TIPS	trauma intervention program
TFC	tactical field care
UEL	upper explosive limit
USAR	urban search and rescue
USCG	United States Coast guard
USPS	United States Postal Service
USSS	United States Secret Service
VX, VE, VG, VM, and VS	V series nerve agents
WMD	weapons of mass destruction
WMD CST	weapons of mass destruction, civil support team
WME	weapons of mass effect

Glossary

Absorption: The process of a substance being taken into the body through the skin (transdermal).

Absorbed Dose: Absorbed dose is the amount of energy deposited in any material by ionizing radiation. The unit of absorbed dose, the rad, is a measure of energy absorbed per gram of material. The unit used in countries other than the U.S. is the gray. One gray equals 100 rad.

Acetylcholine (ACh): The neurotransmitter substance widely distributed throughout the tissues of the body at cholenergic synapses, which causes cardiac inhibition, vasodilatation, gastrointestinal peristalsis, and other parasympathetic effects.

Acetylcholinesterase: An enzyme that hydrolyses the neurotransmitter Acetylcholine. Nerve agents inhibit the action of this enzyme.

Adsorption: The process of a substance becoming chemically attached to a surface.

Agent Dosage: Concentration of a toxic vapor in the air multiplied by the time that the concentration was present.

Air Purification Devices: Respirators or other filtration equipment that remove gases, particulate matter or vapors from the atmosphere.

Airborne Pathogen: Pathological microorganisms spread by droplets expelled or dispersed in the air. While this occurs typically through productive sneezing and/or coughing a deliberate release of pathogens can be accomplished via the use of a variety of aerosol delivery systems.

ALARA: The guiding principle behind radiation protection is that radiation exposures should be kept "As Low As Reasonably Achievable (ALARA)," economic and social factors being taken into account. This common sense approach means that radiation doses for both workers and the public are typically kept lower than their regulatory limits.

Alpha Particle: Alpha particles are composed of two protons and two neutrons. Alpha particles do not travel very far from their radioactive source. They cannot pass through a piece of paper, clothes or even the layer of dead cells which normally protects the skin. Because alpha particles cannot penetrate human skin they are not considered an "external exposure hazard" (this means that if the alpha particles stay outside the human body they cannot harm it). However, alpha particle sources located within the body may pose an "internal" health hazard if they are present in great enough quantities. The risk from indoor radon is due to inhaled alpha particle sources which irradiate lung tissue.

Alkali: Basic compound that possesses the ability to neutralize acids and form a salt.

All Hazards Planning: A fundamental planning approach that takes into account all hazards that a community may need to confront. This is the basic premise of planning and management presently being advocated by FEMA.

Analgesic: A compound capable of producing pain relief without producing anesthesia or loss of consciousness.

Anaphylaxis: An acute, sometimes violent immunological (allergic) reaction characterized by contraction of smooth muscle and dilation of capillaries due to release of pharmacologically active substances (histamines, serotonin). Can be fatal.

Antibody: A component of the immune system, a protein that eliminates or counteracts a foreign substance macromolecule or antigen in the body.

Antidote: A drug or substance that neutralizes a poison or the effects of a poison.

Antigen: Any substance that is capable of inducing an immune response.

APR: Acronym for Air Purifying Respirators

Apnea: Not breathing

Asphyxia: Condition in which cells experience oxygen deprivation.

Assessment: a) Patient assessment—evaluation of patient medical condition. b) Scene assessment—evaluation of the emergency scene which occurs immediately upon arrival and periodically throughout the operation to ensure safety of members, status of activity and to determine extent and implications of response operations.

Ataxia: Inability to coordinate muscle activity during voluntary movement so that smooth movements occur.

Atropine: An anticholinergic medication used as an antidote for nerve agents to counteract excessive amounts of acetylcholine.

Autoignition Temperature: Lowest possible temperature at which a flammable gas or vapor/air mixture will ignite from its own heat source or a contacted heated surface without the necessity of flame or spark.

Autonomic Nervous System: Part of the nervous system controlling involuntary bodily functions; separated into the sympathetic and parasympathetic nervous systems.

Background Radiation: Radiation is a part of our natural world. People have always been exposed to radiation that originates from within the Earth ("terrestrial" sources) and from outer space ("cosmogenic" or "galactic" sources).

Bacteria: Single celled organisms that multiply by cell division and that can cause disease in humans, animals and plants.

Base: *See Alkali*

Beta Particle: Beta particles are similar to electrons except they come from the atomic nucleus and are not bound to any atom. Beta particles cannot travel very far from their radioactive source.

Bio-Terrorism Agent: Living organisms or materials derived from them that cause disease in or injury to humans, animals or plants or cause deterioration of material. Agents can be used in liquid droplet, aerosols or dry powders.

Bio-Terrorism: The deliberate use of biological agents/substances as a weapon to kill or harm humans, animals, plants or to incapacitate equipment.

Binary munition: A chemical munition divided into two sections, each containing precursor chemicals that when combined, release a chemical agent.

BL/P: There are four (4) biosafety levels (BL's) that conform to specified conditions; these conditions consist of a combination of laboratory practices and techniques, safety equipment and laboratory facilities appropriate for the operations performed and the hazards posed by the infectious agents. Previously described as "physical containment (P)" levels.

Blister Agents: A chemical agent which produces local irritation and damage to the skin (vesicant) and mucous membranes, pain and injury to the eyes, reddening and blistering of the skin and damage to the respiratory system when inhaled. Examples are Lewisite, nitrogen mustard and sulfur mustard.

Blood Agent: A chemical agent that is inhaled and absorbed into the blood, acting upon hemoglobin in blood cells. The blood carries the agent to all body tissues where it interferes with the tissue oxygenation process. Examples are cyanogen chloride and hydrogen cyanide.

B-NICE: An acronym for biological, nuclear, incendiary, chemical or explosives.

Body Substance Isolation (BSI): An infection control strategy that considers all body substances potentially infectious, requiring the use of universal precautions.

Boiling Point: Temperature at which a liquid changes its matter state to a gas/vapor. Also the temperature at which the pressure of the liquid equals atmospheric pressure.

Breakthrough Time: The time required for a given chemical to permeate a protective barrier material. This is usually defined as the time elapsed between the application of a chemical to a protective materials exterior surface and its initial appearance on the inner surface.

Brucella: A genus of encapsulated, non-motile bacteria (family Brucellaceae) containing short, rod shaped to coccoid, Gram negative cells. These organisms do not produce gas from carbohydrates, are parasitic, invading all animal tissues and causing infection of the genital organs, mammary gland, and the respiratory and intestinal tracts and are pathogenic for humans and various species of domestic animals.

Bubo: Inflammatory swelling of one or more lymph nodes, usually in the groin; the confluent mass of nodes usually suppurates and drains pus.

CAS Registry Number: A number assigned to a material by the Chemical Abstract Service to provide a single unique identifier.

Causative Agent: The organism or toxin that is responsible for causing a specific disease or harmful effects.

Caustic: A substance that strongly burns, corrodes, irritates or destroys living tissue.

CBR: An acronym for Chemical, Biological and Radiological.

C-cubed I (C3I): A military command term meaning command, control, communications, and intelligence.

Ceiling Exposure Value: The maximum airborne concentration of a biological or chemical agent to which a worker may be exposed at a given time.

Central Nervous System (CNS): Pertaining to the body's central nervous system.

Chemical Agent Symbol: A designation code assigned to a chemical agent which is usually two letters. For example HD Mustard, GB Sarin, CX Phosgene Oxime etc.)

Chemical Degradation: The altering of the chemical structure of a hazardous material usually accomplished during decontamination.

Chemical Protective Ensemble (CPE): Garments specifically designed to protect the eyes and skin from direct chemical contact. There are encapsulating and nonencapsulating versions available for use dependent on the operation and the substance. Garments are usually worn with additional respiratory protection as required.

Chemical Resistance: Ability of the CPE to maintain its protective qualities with it has been contacted by a hazardous substance.

Chemoprophylaxis: Prevention of disease by the use of chemicals or drugs.

Choking Agent: Substances that cause physical injury to the lungs. Exposure is through inhalation. In extreme cases, membranes swell, lungs fill with fluid (edema) with death resulting from lack of oxygen. The victim is "choked." Examples are chlorine and phosgene.

Chronic Exposure: Repeated low dose exposures to a hazardous substance over an extended time frame.

Colorimetric Tubes: Testing mediums that are used to identify the presence and approximated concentration of a substance in the atmosphere.

Combustible Gas Indicator (CGI): Assessment equipment that measures the ambiant concentration of flammable vapors or gases for which it has been set (calibrated) to monitor.

Combustible Liquid: Any liquid that has a flash point at or above 100°F (37.7°C) and below 200°F (93.3°C).

Command: The act of directing, ordering, and/or controlling resources by virtue of explicit legal, agency or delegated authority.

Command Staff: The Command Staff consists of the Safety Officer, Liaison Officer and Public Information Officer who all report directly to the Incident Commander.

Communicable Disease: A disease that can be transmitted from one person to another. Also known as contagious disease.

Communications Failure Protocol: A protocol that dictates agency/unit operations when there is a failure of the telephone and/or EMS radio system.

Communication Order Model: The process of briefly restating an order received to allow for verification and confirmation. This permits all involved to ensure the what was communicated vs. what was heard coincide thus ensuring that the correct action is executed.

Concentration: The amount of a chemical agent present in a unit volume of air, usually expressed in milligrams per cubic meter (mg/m^3).

Concentration Time: The amount of a chemical agent present in a unit volume of air multiplied by the time an individual is exposed to that concentration.

Contagious: Capable of being transmitted from one person to another.

Consequence Management: The measures to alleviate the damage, loss, hardship or suffering caused by emergencies. Consequence management includes measures to protect public health and safety, restore essential government services and provide emergency relief to effected governments, businesses, and individuals. Consequence management is implemented under the primary jurisdiction of the affected State and Local governments. As directed via PDD39 FEMA is designated the lead federal agency for Consequence Management and as such provides support to the State when required.

Contaminant/Contaminated: "A substance or process that poses a threat to life, health or the environment" (NFPA 472).

Corrosives: Substances that destroy the texture or substance of a tissue.

Crisis Management: The measures to identify, acquire and plan the use of resources needed to anticipate, prevent and/or resolve a terrorist threat or incident. As directed via PDD39 the FBI is designated the lead federal agency for Consequence Management. Crisis Management is implemented under the direction of the FBI.

Culture: A population of microorganisms grown in a medium.

Cumulative: Additional exposure rather then repeated exposure. The collective effect of having an HD exposure for 30 minutes and several hours later being exposed again for 60 minutes would yield the same effect as a single 90-minute exposure.

Cutaneous: Pertaining to the skin.

Cyanosis: A dark bluish or purplish coloration of the skin and mucous membranes due to deficient oxygen levels in the blood (hypoxia). Presence is evident when reduced hemoglobin in the blood exceeds 5g per 100 ml.

Decontamination (decon): The removal of contamination from responders, patients, vehicles, and equipment. Patients must be decontaminated before treatment/transport. Usually accomplished through a physical or chemical process.

Dermal: The skin or derma

Dermis: The inner layer of the skin, beneath the epidermis, which contains blood vessels, nerves and structures of the skin.

Desortion: The reverse process of absorption. The agent will be "removed" from the surface, outgassing.

Dilution Factor: Dilution of contaminated air with uncontaminated air in a general area, room, or building for the purpose of health hazard or nuisance control, and/or for heating and cooling.

Disaster Cache: A store of pre-determined supplies/equipment that is immediately transported to an MCI or disaster.

Disaster-Catastrophic Incidents/Events: An MCI that overwhelms both local and regional response capabilities and typically involves multiple overlapping jurisdictional boundaries and requiring significant multi-jurisdictional response and coordination.

Diseases: An alteration of health, with a characteristic set of symptoms, which may affect the entire body or specific organs. Diseases have a variety of causes and are known as infectious diseases when due to a pathogenic microorganism such as a bacteria, virus, or fungus.

Division/Branch: The organizational level having functional or geographic responsibility for major segments of incident operations. The branch level is organizationally between section and group/sector.

DMAT: Disaster Medical Assistance Team; a deployable team (usually 35 people) of medical personnel and support units under the command of the Office of Emergency Preparedness, U.S. Public Health Service.

DNA: Deoxyribonucleic acid: the genetic material of all organisms and viruses (except for a small class of RNA-containing viruses) that code structures and materials used in normal metabolism.

Dosage: a) The proper therapeutic amount of a drug to be administered to a patient. b) The concentration of a chemical agent in the atmosphere (C) multiplied by the time (t) the concentration remains, expressed as mg-min/m. The dosage (Ct) received by a person depends on how long they are exposed to the concentration. That is, the respiratory dosage in mg-min/m is equal to the time in minutes an individual is unmasked in an agent cloud multiplied by the concentration of the cloud. The dosage is equal to the time of exposure in minutes of an individual's unprotected skin multiplied by the concentration of the agent cloud.

Downwind Distance: The distance a toxic agent vapor cloud will travel from its point of origin with the wind.

Dyspnea: Shortness of breath, breathing distress.

Edema: An accumulation of an excessive amount of watery fluid in cells, tissues or serous cavities.

Electron: Electrons are very small particles with a single negative charge. They are a part of the atom and orbit around the nucleus. Electrons are much smaller than protons or neutrons. The mass of an electron is only about one two-thousandth of a proton or neutron.

Emergency Operations Center (EOC): A central disaster management center staffed by representatives from response and support agencies.

Emergency Operations Plan (EOP): An operational document that has resulted in the delineation of response plans for a community or organization. This plan is usually the result of issues that have been identified through a threat assessment survey.

Emergency Support Functions (ESF): Support functions outlined in the Federal Response Plan. ESF's identify lead and secondary agencies, and are not a management system. The ESF's are grouped by 12 identified functional tasks. ESF #1 Transportation, #2 Communications, #3 Public Works and Engineering, #4 Fire-fighting, #6 Mass Care, #7 Resource Support (Logistics), #8 Health and medical services, #9 USAR, #10 Hazardous Materials, #11 Food, #12 Energy

Epidermis: The outer layer of skin

Equivalent Dose: The equivalent dose is a measure of the effect which radiation has on humans. The concept of equivalent dose involves the impact that different types of radiation have on humans. Not all types of radiation produce the same effect in humans. The equivalent dose takes into account the type of radiation and the absorbed dose. For example when considering beta, x-ray, and gamma ray radiation, the equivalent dose (expressed in rems) is equal to the absorbed dose (expressed in rads). For alpha radiation, the equivalent dose is assumed to be twenty times the absorbed dose.

Etiological Agent: A living organism that may cause human disease (NFPA 472).

Evaporation Rate: The rate at which a liquid changes to vapor at normal room temperature.

Exothermic Reaction: A chemical reaction that produces heat.

Explosive Range: *See Flammable Range*

Facilities Unit: Responsible for support facilities, including shelter, rehabilitation, sanitation, and auxiliary power.

Fasciculation: Involuntary contractions or twitching of groups (fasciculi) of muscle fibers, a coarser form of muscular contraction than fibrillation. Commonly described as the movement resembling a "bag of worms."

Federal Coordinating Officer (FCO): Is the President of the United States representative at a disaster incident. For the purposes of this textbook, the FCO is the individual responsible for coordinating the consequence management response and will usually be a representative of FEMA.

Federal Emergency Management Agency: Is the lead Federal agency for the consequence management response to a terrorism incident as directed via PDD39 and the FRP.

Federal Response Plan (FRP): The FRP provides the system for the overall delivery of Federal assistance in a disaster. 27 Federal departments and agencies and the American Red Cross provide resources. Resources are grouped into 12 Emergency Support Functions (ESF's) each headed by a primary or lead Agency. For the purposes of this textbook, the FRP presents the Federal Government's consequence management response to terrorism incidents.

Finance/Administration Section: The unit responsible for all costs and financial actions of the incident and administrative functions, which includes the Time Unit, Procurement Unit, Compensation/Claims Unit and Cost Unit.

Flammability: The inherent capacity of a substance to ignite and burn rapidly.

Flammable Range: Range of a gas or vapor concentration that will burn or explode if an ignition source is present. Usually expressed in percentage by volume of air. Dependent on range there are lower explosive limits (LEL) and upper explosive limits (UEL). For an ignition to take place the substance must be within the LEL & UEL. Any presences that does not meet or exceeds these ranges should not ignite.

Flash Point: Minimum temperature at which a liquid gives off sufficient enough vapor to ignite and flash over but not continue to burn without the availability of more heat.

G Series Nerve Agents: Chemical agents with moderate to high toxicity that act by inhibiting a key nervous system enzyme developed in the 1930's. (GA, GB, GD)

Gamma Rays: Gamma rays are an example of electromagnetic radiation, as is visible light. Gamma rays originate from the nucleus of an atom. They are capable of traveling long distances through air and most other materials. Gamma rays require more "shielding" material, such as lead or steel, to reduce their numbers than is required for alpha and beta particles.

Group/Sector: The organizational level having responsibility for a specified functional assignment at an incident (triage, treatment, extrication, etc.).

Half-life: The time required for the level of a substance to be reduced by 50% of its initial level.

High Impact Incident/Event: Any emergency that would require the access of mutual aid resources in order to effectively manage the incident or to maintain community 911 operations.

Host: A person that can harbor or nourish a disease producing organism. The host is infected.

Hydration: The combining of a substance with water.

Hydrolysis: The reaction of any chemical substance with water by which decomposition of the substance occurs and one or more new substances are produced.

Hypoxia: A condition when insufficient oxygen is available to meet the oxygen demands of the cells.

Hypoxemia: The reduction of oxygen content in the arterial blood.

IDLH: Immediate Danger to Life and Health.

Idiopathic: Referring to a disease of unknown origin

Immunization: The process of rendering a person immune or highly resistant to a disease. Usually accomplished through vaccination.

Immunoassay: Detection and assay of substances by serological (immunological) methods; in most applications the substance in question serves as antigen, both in antibody production and in measurement of antibody by the test substance.

Incapacitating Agents: Substances that produce temporary physiological and/or mental effects via action on the central nervous system. Effects may persist for hours or days but victims usually do not require medical treatment although treatment will assist in speeding recovery.

Incendiary Device: A device designed to start a fire

Incident Action Plan: A plan consisting of the strategic goals, tactical objectives and support requirements for the incident. All incidents require an action plan. For simple/smaller incidents that action plan is not usually in written form. Larger or complex responses require the action plan to be documented in writing.

Incident Command Post (ICP): The location from which Command functions are executed.

Incident Management System (IMS): Originally known as the Incident Command System, IMS has evolved into a systematic management approach with a common organizational structure responsible for the management of assigned resources to effectively accomplish stated objectives pertaining to an incident.

Incident Manager (IM): The designated person with overall authority for management of the incident (varies by jurisdiction).

Incident Objectives: Statements of guidance and direction necessary for the selection of appropriate strategy(s) and the tactical direction of resources to accomplish the same. Incident objectives are based on realistic expectations of operational accomplishments when all anticipated resources have been deployed. Incident objectives must be achievable and measurable, yet flexible enough to allow for strategic and tactical realignment.

Incident Termination/Securement: The conclusion of emergency operations at the scene of an incident, usually the departure of the last resource from the incident scene.

Incubation Period: The time from exposure to the disease until the first appearance of symptoms.

Infection: Growth of pathogenic organisms in the tissues of a host, with or without detectable signs of injury.

Infectious: Capable of causing infection in a suitable host.

Infectious Disease: An illness or disease resulting from invasion of a host by disease-producing organisms such as bacteria, viruses, fungi or parasites.

Infectivity: a) The ability of an organism to spread. b) The number of organisms required to cause an infection to secondary hosts. c) The capabilities of an organism to spread out from site of infection and cause disease in the host organism. Infectivity also can be defined as the number of organisms required to cause an infection.

Ingestion: Exposure to a substance through the gastrointestinal tract.

Inhalation: Exposure to a substance through the respiratory tract.

Injection: Exposure to a substance through a break in the skin.

Inoculation: *See Vaccine*

Ions, Ionization: Atoms which have the same number of electrons and protons have zero charge since the number of positively charged protons equals the number of negatively charged electrons. If an atom has more electrons than protons, it has a negative charge, and is called a negative ion. Atoms which have fewer electrons than protons are positively charged, and are called positive ions. Some forms of radiation can strip electrons from atoms. This type of radiation is appropriately called "ionizing radiation."

Ionizing Radiation: Ionizing radiation is radiation that has enough energy to cause atoms to lose electrons and become ions. Alpha and beta particles, as well as gamma and x-rays, are all examples of ionizing radiation. Ultraviolet, infrared, and visible light are examples of nonionizing radiation.

Law Enforcement Incident Command System (LEICS): A law enforcement incident management system based on the IMS model.

LD$_{50}$: Dose (LD is lethal dose) that will kill 50% of the exposed population.

LEL: Lower Explosive Limit. The minimum concentration of a substance (gas or vapor) is required for a substance to burn.

Level A Protection: The level of protective equipment in situations where the substance is considered acutely vapor toxic to the skin and the hazards are unknown. Use of Level is recommended when immediate identification of the substance is unavailable or unknown. Level A consists of a full encapsulating protective ensemble with SCBA or SABA.

Level B Protection: The level of protective equipment in situations where the substance is considered acutely vapor toxic to the skin and the hazards may cause respiratory effects. Level B consists of a level B encapsulating (non-airtight) protective ensemble or chemical splash suit with SCBA or SABA.

Level C Protection: The level of protective equipment required to prevent respiratory exposure but not to exclude possible skin contact. Chemical splash suits with cartridge respirators (APR's).

Level D Protection: The level of protective equipment required when the atmosphere contains no known hazard, when splashes, immersions, inhalation, or contact with hazardous levels of any substance is precluded. Work uniform such as coveralls, boots, leather gloves and hard hat.

Liaison: The coordination of activities between agencies operating at the incident.

Liaison Officer: The point of contact (POC) for assisting or coordinating agencies and members of the Management Staff. The Liaison Officer is a member of the Management Staff.

Liquid Agent: Chemical agent that appears to be an oily film or droplet form. Color usually brownish in color.

Logistics Section: The section responsible for providing facilities, services, and materials for the incident, which includes the Communication Unit, Medical Unit, and Food Unit within the Service Branch; and the Supply Unit, Facilities Unit and Ground Support Unit within the Support Branch.

Low Impact Incident/Event: An MCI that can be managed by local EMS resources and members without mutual aid resources from outside organizations.

Macula: A small spot, perceptibly different in color from surrounding skin.

Mass Casualty Incident (MCI): An incident with several patients or an unusual event associated with minimal casualties (airplane crash, terrorism, haz mat, etc.); incident with negative impact on hospitals, EMS, and response resources.

Mass Decontamination: The decontamination of mass numbers of patients (pediatric, adult, and geriatric) from exposure to radiation, or a chemical/biological agent.

Mechanism of Injury: A sudden and intense energy transmitted to the body that causes trauma or exposure to a chemical or biological agent. A contaminated patient can transport a chem-bio mechanism of injury.

Median Incapacitating Dosage (ID50): The amount of liquid chemical agent expected to incapacitate 50% of a group exposed, unprotected individuals.

Median Lethal Dosage (LCT50): The amount of liquid chemical agent expected to kill 50% of a group of exposed, unprotected individuals.

Medium: Substance used to provide nutrients for the growth and multiplication of microorganisms.

Minor Patient: A patient with minor injuries that requires minimal treatment; triage color is green.

Mitigation: Actions taken to prevent or reduce the likelihood of harm.

Mists: Liquid droplets dispersed in the air.

M8 Chemical Agent Detector Paper: A paper used to detect and identify liquid V and G class nerve agents and H class blis).

Physiological Action: Most toxic chemical agents are used for their toxic effect. The effects are the production of harmful physiological reactions when the human body is exposed either through external, inhalation or internal routes. The subsequent bodily response to the exposure is the physiological response.

Poison: Any substance which, taken into the body by absorption, ingestion, inhalation, or injection and interferes with normal physiological functions.

Post Incident Analysis (PIA): A written review of major incidents for the purpose of implementing changes in operations, resources, logistics, and protocols, based on lessons learned.

ppm: Parts per million

Precursor: A chemical substance required for the manufacture of chemical agents.

Prophylaxis: Prevention of disease or of a process that can lead to a disease.

Proton: Protons, along with neutrons, make up the nucleus of an atom. Protons have a single positive charge. While protons and neutrons are about 2,000 times heavier than electrons, they are still very small particles. A grain of sand weighs about a hundred million trillion (100,000,000,000,000,000,000) times more than a proton or a neutron.

Psychochemical Agent: Chemical agent that incapacitates by distorting the perceptions and cognitive processes of the victim.

Public Information Officer (PIO): The person responsible for interface with the media and others requiring information direct from the incident scene. Information is only disseminated with the authorization of the Incident Commander. The PIO is a member of the Command Staff.

Pull Logistics: A process of ordering supplies by field units, via communications, as they are needed at an MCI or disaster.

Pulmonary Edema: Edema of the lungs. Left unattended in severe cases can be fatal.

Push Logistics: A process of forwarding pre-determined supplies, usually as a disaster cache, to an MCI or disaster.

Radiation: Radiation is energy in the form of waves or particles (see types of radiation). Radiation comes from sources such as radioactive material or from equipment such as X-ray machines, or accelerators.

Radiation Dose: The effect of radiation on any material is determined by the "dose" of radiation that material receives. Radiation dose is simply the quantity of radiation energy deposited in a material. There are several terms used in radiation protection to precisely describe the various aspects associated with the concept of dose and how radiation energy deposited in tissue affects humans.

Radiation Exposure: Radiation exposure is a measure of the amount of ionization produced by x-rays or gamma rays as they travel through air. The unit of radiation exposure is the roentgen (R), named for Wilhelm Roentgen, the German scientist who in 1895 discovered x-rays.

Radiation Half-Life: The time required for a population of atoms of a given radionuclide to decrease, by radioactive decay, to exactly one-half of its original number is called the radionuclide's half-life. No operation, either chemical or physical, can change the decay rate of a radioactive substance. Half-lives range from much less than a microsecond to more than a billion years. The longer the half-life the more stable the nuclide. After one half-life, half the original atoms will remain; after two half-lives, one fourth (or 1/2 of 1/2) will remain; after three half-lives one eighth of the original number (1/2 of 1/2 of 1/2) will remain; and so on.

Radiation Meters: Monitoring devices that detect, measure and monitor for the presence of radiation.

Radioactive Contamination: Radioactive contamination is radioactive material distributed over some area, equipment or person. It tends to be unwanted in the location where it is, and has to be cleaned up or decontaminated.

Radioactive Decay: Radioactive decay describes the process where an energetically unstable atom transforms itself to a more energetically favorable, or stable, state. The unstable atom can emit ionizing radiation in order to become more stable. This atom is said to be "radioactive", and the process of change is called "radioactive decay".

Rate of Action: Rate at which the body reacts to or is affected by a chemical substance.

Reactivity: Ability of a substance to interact with other substances and/or body tissues.

Resource Status Unit (RESTAT): The unit within the Planning Section responsible for recording the status of, and accounting for, resources committed to the incident, and for evaluation of a.) Resources currently committed to the incident, b.) The impact that additional responding units will have on an incident, and lastly, anticipated resource requirements. Note: RESTAT is normally utilized at actual or escalating high impact or long term operations.

Rickettsia: Generic name applied to a group of microorganisms, family Rickettsiaceae, order Rickettsiales, which occupy a position intermediate between viruses and bacteria. They are the causative agents of many diseases and are usually transmitted by lice, fleas, ticks, and mites (arthropods).

Riot Control Agents: Substances usually having short term effects that are typically used by governmental authorities for law enforcement purposes.

Routes of Exposure: The mechanism by which a contaminant enters the body.

SABA: Supplied Air Breathing Apparatus

Safety Officer: The Command Staff member responsible for monitoring and assessing safety hazards, unsafe situations and developing measures for ensuring member safety on-site.

Sarin: A nerve poison which is an extremely potent irreversible cholinesterase inhibitor.

SCBA: Self-Contained Breathing Apparatus

Secondary Device: The employment of a second attack device in order to yield injury and death upon responders.

Section: The organizational level having functional responsibility for primary segments of incident operations such as Operations, Planning, Logistics and Finance/Administration. The section level is organizationally between Branch and Incident Commander.

Section Chief: Title referring to a member of the General Staff (Operations Section Chief, Planning Section Chief, Logistics Section Chief and Finance/Administration Section Chief).

Sector/Group Officer: The individual responsible for supervising members who are performing a similar function or task (i.e.: triage, treatment, transport or extrication).

Security Unit: Responsible for personnel security, traffic control, and morgue security at an MCI or disaster.

Sensitize: To become highly responsive (sensitive) or easily receptive to the effects of a toxic substance after initial exposure.

Sequala (ae): A condition following as a consequence of a disease.

Shigellosis: Bacillary dysentery caused by a bacteria of the genus Shigella, often occurring in epidemic patterns.

Short Term Exposure Limits (STEL): A 15 minute time weighted average (TWA) exposure which should not be exceeded at any time during a work day even if the 8 hour TWA is within the threshold limit value (TLV). Exposures at the STEL should not be repeated more then four times a day and there should be at least 60 minutes between successive exposures at the STEL.

Situation Status Unit (SITSTAT): The Unit within the Planning Section responsible for analysis of the situation as it progresses, reporting to the Planning Section

Chief. Note: SITSTAT is normally utilized at actual or escalating high impact or long term operations.

Skin Dosage: Equal to the time of exposure in minutes of an individuals unprotected skin multiplied by the concentration of the agent cloud.

Sloughing: Process by which necrotic cells separate from the tissues to which they have been attached.

Solubility: a) Ability of a material (solid, liquid, gas, or vapor) to dissolve in a solvent. b) Ability of one material to blend uniformly with another.

Solvent: Material that is capable of dissolving another chemical.

Soman: An extremely potent cholinesterase inhibitor.

Span of Control: The number of subordinates supervised by a superior; ideal span varies from three to five people.

Specific Gravity: Weight of a liquid compared to the weight of an equal volume of water.

Spore: A reproductive form some microorganisms can take to become resistant to environmental conditions such as cold or heat. This is referred to as the "resting phase."

Staging: A specific status where resources are assembled in an area at or near the incident scene to await deployment or assignment.

Staging Area: The location where incident personnel and equipment are assigned on an immediately available status.

START: Acronym for Simple Treatment And Rapid Treatment. This is an initial triage system utilized for triaging large numbers of patients at an emergency incident. This system was developed in Newport Beach, California in the early 80's.

Strike Team: Up to five of the same kind or type of resource with common communications and an assigned leader.

Supply Unit: The unit within the Support Branch of the Logistics Section responsible for providing the personnel, equipment and supplies to support incidents operations.

Tactical Objectives: The specific operations that must be accomplished to achieve strategic goals. Tactical objectives must be specific and measurable, and are usually accomplished at the division or group level.

Technical Advisor: Any individual with specialized expertise useful to the management/general staff.

Technical Specialists: Personnel with special skills who are activated only when needed. Technical specialists may be needed in the areas of rescue, water resources, and training. Technical Specialists report initially to the Planning Section, but may be assigned anywhere within the IMS organizational structure as needed.

Teratogenicity: Capacity of a substance to produce fetal malformation.

Time Weighted Averages (TWA): Average concentration for a normal 8 hour work day and a 40 hour work week to which nearly all workers may be repeatedly exposed without adversity.

Toxicity: Property a substance possesses which enables it to injure the physiological mechanism of an organism by chemical means with the maximum effect being incapacitation or death. The relative toxicity of an agent can be articulated in milligrams of toxin needed per kilogram of body weight to kill experimental animals.

Toxins: Poisonous substances produced by living organisms.

Transfer of Command: A process of transferring command responsibilities from one individual to another. Commonly a formal procedure conducted in a face to face interaction with a event synopsis briefing and completed by a radio transmission announcing that a certain individual is now assuming command responsibility of an incident. A similar transition occurs when a sector/group or division/branch transfers responsibilities.

UEL: Upper Explosive Limits

Unified Command: A standard method to coordinate command of an incident when multiple agencies have either functional or geographical jurisdiction. This results in a command system with shared responsibility.

Unity of Command: The concept of an individual being a supervisor at each level of the IMS, beginning at the unit level, and extending upward to the incident manager.

Universal Precautions: "System of infectious disease control which assumes that direct contact with body fluids is infectious." (OSHA) Centers for Disease Control and Injury Prevention have published a series of procedures and precaution guidelines to assist the rescuer in fully understanding threat potential and protective measures required.

Upwind: In or toward the direction from which the wind blows. Placing yourself with the wind blowing towards the suspected release site.

Urticaria: Skin condition characterized by intensely itching red, raised patches of skin.

USAR: Urban Search And Rescue

US DOT Hazard Classifications: Hazard class designations for specific hazardous materials as delineated in the US DOT Regulations.

V Series Nerve Agents: Generally persistent chemical agents of moderate to high toxicity developed in the 1950's that act by inhibiting a key nervous system enzyme. Examples are VX, VE, VG, VM, and VS.

Vaccine: A preparation of a killed or weakened microorganism products used to artificially induce immunity against a disease.

Vapors: Gaseous form of a substance that is normally a liquid or a solid state at room temperature and pressure.

Vapor Agent: A gaseous form of a chemical agent. If heavier than air, the cloud will be down to the ground, if lighter than air the cloud will rise and dissipate more quickly.

Vapor Density: A comparison of any gas or vapor to the weight of an equal amount of air.

Vesicant Agent: *See Blister Agent*

Virulence: The disease-evoking power of a microorganism in a given host.

Virus: A microorganism usually only visible with an electron microscope. Viruses normally reside within other living (host) cells, and cannot reproduce outside of a living cell. It is an infectious microorganism that exists as a particle rather than as a complete cell. Particle sizes range from 200 to 400 nanometers (one billionth of a meter).

Viscosity: Degree to which a fluid resists flow.

Volatility: Measure of how readily a substance will vaporize.

Vomiting Agent: Substance that produces nausea and vomiting effects. Can also cause coughing, sneezing, pain in the nose and throat, nasal discharge and tears.

Water Reactive: Any substance that readily reacts with or decomposes in the presence of water with a significant energy release.

Water Solubility: Quantity of a chemical substance that will dissolve or mix with water.

Weapons of Mass Destruction (WMD): Weaponization of nuclear, radiological, biological or chemical substances.

Weapons of Mass Effect (WME): Same definition as WMD but reflects a more accurate description of the events surrounding use of these type weapons. Destruction is not guaranteed when utilized but societal effect in many ways can be assured.

X-Rays: X-rays are an example of electromagnetic radiation which arises as electrons are deflected from their original paths or inner orbital electrons change their orbital levels around the atomic nucleus. X-rays, like gamma rays are capable of traveling long distances through air and most other materials. Like gamma rays, X-rays require more shielding to reduce their intensity than do beta or alpha particles. X- and gamma rays differ primarily in their origin: x-rays originate in the electronic shell, gamma rays originate in the nucleus.

Contact Information and References:

CDC—888-232-3228

National Response Center—800-424-8802

NDMS—800-USA-NDMS

Nuclear Regulatory Commission—301-492-7000

DoD Joint Nuclear Accident Center—703-325-2102

INTERNET REFERENCES:

CDC   http://www.bt.cdc.gov/

DOE   http://www.dp.doe.gov/

EPA   http://www.epa.gov/swercepp

FBI   http://www.fbi.gov

FEMA   http://www.fema.gov

FEMA: Terrorist Incident Planning Guidelines
             http://www.fema.gov/pte/pte052101.htm

HHS OEP   http://oep.dhhs.gov/

NDPO   http://www.ndpo.gov

NGB   http://www.ngb.dtic.mil

DOJ ODP   http://www.ojp.usdoj.gov/odp/

SBCCOM   http://www.sbccom.army.mil/

OTHERS:

George Washington University ASAP Center—http://www.gwumc.edu/asap/

RAND   http://www.RAND.org

CBACI   http://www.cbaci.org

The Center for Strategic & International Studies   http://www.csis.org

Harvard University Kennedy School of Government—
Executive Session of Domestic Preparedness
http://ksgnotes1.harvard.edu/BCSIA/ESDP.nsf/www/Home